To my

Be Blessed

As you Read!

Wayne Johnson

bwaynej@gmail.com

Out of My Mind

AND

Heart

Creative Insights to
Biblical Passages

WAYNE JOHNSON

FOREWORD

I have been a student of the Bible for many years. Its writings continue to fascinate me, as well as call me to a life of deep spiritual examination. I have taught adult Bible classes and preached its message for over 50 years.

The entries in this book are a compilation of writings I have done over the course of a few years. The thoughts expressed are entirely my own, and are based mainly on passages of Scripture from the Bible, a good many from the Psalms. Interspersed among these are poems I have written.

There is no particular organization to the writings. They may be read in any order. It is my intention that the ideas presented would be helpful in understanding Scripture, as well as serving to undergird the faith of those who read them.

The photos placed between articles are original photos I have taken, as are many embedded within the written pieces themselves. Other photos are used by permission.

Scripture references are from the English Standard Version (ESV) unless otherwise noted: King James Version (KJV), The Message Bible. Most Scripture passages are in italics.

CONTENTS

1.

A DIFFERENT JESUS
– Rev. 1:12-18

"Then I turned to see the voice that was speaking to me, and on turning I saw seven golden lampstands, and in the midst of the lampstands one like a son of man, clothed with a long robe and with a golden sash around his chest. The hairs of his head were white, like white wool, like snow. His eyes were like a flame of fire, his feet were like burnished bronze, refined in a furnace, and his voice was like the roar of many waters. In his right hand he held seven stars, from his mouth came a sharp two-edged sword, and his face was like the sun shining in full strength. When I saw him, I fell at his feet as though dead. But he laid his right hand on me, saying, 'Fear not…'"

The apostle John's world was about to be turned upside down. He was living in exile on the island of Patmos when a vision of a man exploded before his eyes. Was this Jesus? Not the Jesus he thought he knew.

In the Gospel accounts, John had related to Jesus as one man to another man. But suddenly, here, in this encounter with the image before him, John was instead stunned, overwhelmed to the point of feeling physically assaulted. He could only fall to the ground as if life had been drained out of him. Where was the Jesus he had known in Galilee – a man, fully human, with Galilean clothes, sweaty brow, bearded, maybe with dirty hands and oily face? He couldn't even tell if there was a friendly smile on his face because of the brilliance of Jesus' countenance.

What images of Jesus had John carried for perhaps some sixty years? Certainly, a teacher extraordinaire, a miracle worker, the crucified, tortured body on a cross, the resurrected Jesus appearing suddenly in a closed room, an ascending Lord – all were fixed pictures in John's mind. Those impressions carried him for many years. In the beginning, John had seen Jesus as a rabbi, like other rabbis in Judea. Gradually, he became deeply aware that this man Jesus was something more, manifestly different from all other rabbis.

After the resurrection, John and the other disciples saw a Jesus who was remarkably different, yet still had the same physical characteristics: the body and face were recognizable, and even the dreadful marks of crucifixion were still visible. But amazingly, he could appear and disappear at will, even coming through a closed door! In their three years of exposure to him, Jesus had never done that before. And later, on a lakeshore in Galilee, John, with the other disciple fishermen, could still recognize that that figure standing on the beach was indeed Jesus.

At Jesus' ascension, John would have seen the same Jesus he had known for three years. Standing on a Mount of Olives hillside, John had no doubt who it was as they saw him ascend into the clouds. Over the years since that event, John's fellowship with Jesus would operate in a spiritual realm, as would be true for all Jesus' followers: praying in Jesus' name, teaching the Word of Jesus to the growing churches, observation of Jesus acting in John's and other's lives. He would have savored the sense of Jesus' presence with him.

But now, on Patmos, this Jesus presented a fiery, awesome persona: glorious Lord of all. It was physically painful to stand and look on his face, a face like the sun blazing in full strength.

John's image of Jesus had to undergo a dramatic revision. This One before him now was absolutely different. The overwhelming splendor and glory of Jesus was unimaginable, not at all like the Galilean teacher and miracle worker he was accustomed to.

John's vision of a different Jesus came only through revelation. It was given to him. He could never have conjured it up in his mind. His experience is emblematic of what all believers must go through. Like John, I may have found my image of Jesus shifting over the years. I am familiar with the words of the Gospels. I've read about Jesus, observed his image in those pages. Maybe I have struggled to connect those images, concepts and ideas with a living person. Who is Jesus to me? Is he simply a concept, a disembodied spirit?

I may never have the revelation that John did, ending up falling stunned at Jesus' feet. But may it not be true for me, that in my contemplation of Jesus, I am gaining a new image of him in my spirit? The Apostle Paul says we are being changed *"from one degree of glory to another"* as we *"behold the glory of the Lord"* (2 Corinthians 3:18). Certainly, that change will involve newer and greater understandings of who Jesus is. The Jesus I knew in the beginning of my Christian walk becomes more glorious and real. The Jesus I see in eternity will be closer to the image John saw on the island of Patmos.

But how does a person develop a new and deeper awareness, a new and different image of Jesus? It must come as a gift from him. I can ask for it. I am dull of heart, to be sure. But I am certain the Father must be delighted to reveal his Son to me in greater and greater glory, leading me further and further toward that final view I will have of him.

"Before the mountains were brought forth,
or ever you had formed the earth and the world,
from everlasting to everlasting you are God"
Psalm 90:2

2.
HE IS THERE AND HE DOES THINGS!

1. A DISCOVERY

One of our enduring questions as Christians is how God works in the world, more specifically, in our personal world. What is he up to? Can we identify where he is at work in us and through us? What is termed God's providence can be spoken of as his ways in this world, where his actions intersect with our own. Questions about prayer have particular relevance: does God answer prayer? The Bible directs us to request in prayer that God act. But why do we not see more connection between our praying and his responses? Mystery attends any thoughts of God's providential acts. Yet Scripture makes plain that God is indeed at work in his world. Scripture also affirms that we should expect to observe God in his works.

I can attest to a number of interventions by God. The first occurred while I was pastoring in northern Wisconsin. With John, a fellow-pastor, I was returning from a hunting trip in Montana. That day, as we crossed North Dakota on I-90, I drove while John slept. I remember it as a sunny day. It was quiet in the car, and I was musing about my spiritual life as I drove. For a while I had been feeling quite discouraged, even depressed, over my connection with God. Where was the sense of his presence? I didn't seem to experience Christ very deeply. Why was I not more fervent in spiritual disciplines? Where was the zeal to do the will of God?

I was expressing these thoughts to the Lord as I drove. Suddenly, there popped into my head these lines:

> *"Speak to Him, for He listens,*
>
> *And Spirit with spirit can meet;*
>
> *Closer is He than breathing,*
>
> *Nearer than hands and feet."*

The words startled me, for they seemed directed from heaven, just what I needed to hear. They sounded vaguely familiar, though I wasn't sure where I had heard them. I could not identify them as a Bible passage. Anyway, the lines were a tremendous comfort to me. Christ was close: that was the message. He was nearer than hands and feet, even breathing. I fed on those words for many days. But I was curious, intrigued by where the lines came from. So, I asked God to help me find out who wrote them. (This was long before Google could search out anything.) While studying some printed material for teaching our youth, I noticed the writer had quoted those lines that came to me while traveling through North Dakota. But he hadn't cited the author! I wrote the publisher, asking for the source of those words (this was pre-email). They responded but their answer was most discouraging: they didn't know where the verse came from either. I earnestly told the Lord that I really wanted to know the source. Time passed. One day I happened to be browsing in the local library, though not sure now for what reason. At random, I was moving down stacks of books and ended up in the poetry section. Again, at random, I picked up a poetry book, which happened to be poems by Alfred Lord Tennyson. I began paging through the book, glancing at poems. Wonder of wonders, there on one page of the book were those poetic lines in a piece called The Higher Pantheon. I couldn't believe how it happened! Clearly, without doubt, God had guided me to the source of the lines. It was an act of kindness on his part. I was thrilled! Alfred Lord Tennyson had written them. The God of the universe did not need to stoop to fulfil that rather mundane request of mine but he did.

2. ANOTHER KINDNESS

The year was 1985, Christmas time. I had been alone in Seattle looking for a job since the end of September. At the time, I was staying by myself in a house owned by a man from the church I attended. He worked out-state, and intending to sell the house, wanted someone to "house-sit". As the holiday season approached, I desperately wanted to go home to my family in Wisconsin. So, I booked a flight to Minneapolis. But as the time for departure arrived, flights were being delayed, day after day. The whole area, including the airport, was fogged in. No planes could land. The fog lasted for many days, with no prospect of a change.

On the morning of my flight, I was at a loss as to what to do. Desperately I cried out to the Lord: "I don't care what your will is; I just want to go home!" It was not the way I should address God, with such insolence. He didn't rebuke me. At that point, I called the airline, Northwest Orient, and asked what I should do. The service representative confirmed that no activity was taking place, no planes landing or taking off. She said if I wished, I could come down to the airport and just wait. I decided that was my only choice, hopeless as it was.

At the terminal I walked to my assigned gate. (This was before TSA and security checks!) I found a chair and just waited. The runways were quite invisible, with fog blanketing the whole area. No planes were moving anywhere. I waited. And waited. And waited. Suddenly I noticed the fog lifting, the sun beaming through, and quickly four planes landed as fast as they could. And just as suddenly, after only 10 minutes, the fog closed in again. But I didn't think much of it. I just waited.

In a few minutes, a huge Boeing 747 nosed up to the gate where I waited. Again, at first, I didn't think anything of it. Finally, I walked to the desk and asked the attendant, "Is that my plane, going to Minneapolis?" She replied, "It is!" Well, what was I to think now? I recall just being sort of numb, not fully understanding what was happening. Then I happened to overhear two nearby pilots talking. They were evidently waiting to take the 747 on to Minneapolis. One said to the other, "Do you see that 747 there? It came from Tokyo, planned to refuel here in Seattle but could not land because of the fog. So, it flew on to Moses Lake to refuel. (Moses Lake was a Boeing training airport in interior Washington state.) After refueling, and taking off, the plane received a radio message saying there was the possibility of a break in the clouds and fog in Seattle. The pilots reversed course, headed back to Seattle, and landed in that break in the clouds." It was that short break which I had observed. I was stunned! That was my plane that had bypassed Seattle, but God turned it around and brought it back, having opened a hole in the clouds that allowed the plane to land. How kind of God! He did not rebuke my petulant outburst but graciously granted my need to go home.

3. A REVELATION

How does a person understand the love of God for us? Many Christians claim his love is unconditional. But their behavior and manner of thinking frequently contradicts their beliefs. In other words, in their heart of hearts,

God's love is indeed conditional. It depends on one's conduct. It can ebb and flow. If I order my life aright, not sinning, but being faithful to try and serve God, God's love flows over me and I have a sense of well-being. But when I am conscious of some sin in my life, or of not having some useful function to God, he is of course displeased and disappointed.

In the late 1990's I discovered there was a disconnect between what I believed biblically and what I believed in my heart of hearts. I knew God's love was unconditional. Of course. I knew it scripturally and theologically. I had taught it and preached it. But over a period of time, I realized I didn't actually believe it. It hit me that my view of God's love was that he loved me for what he could get out of me. That is, if I was spiritually productive in behavior and in service to God, he would love me. Where that was absent, then not so much. If I was faithful in spiritual disciplines, I could count on his love. My reality was God did not love me for myself alone. What if I never did anything for him? Would he love me just as much? I could not answer that question positively. What if there were huge flaws in my spiritual life, huge gaps in spiritual maturity? Would God love me just as much? Again, I could not answer Yes.

Late one night, about 11:00, under a darkened sky, I found myself stand-ing in my backyard, alone, mulling over the thought God did not love me for myself alone but only for what I could do for him. Spontaneously, with no forethought, I burst out audibly, "God, if you love me, flash a meteor across the sky." Immediately, within a second or two, a bright flaming meteor dashed across my view, from north to south. I was stunned! In fact, breathless! How could this happen, that I merely ask for a meteor to show and it does?

What kind of a God is this who responds to such seemingly frivolous requests? Later, in thinking about my actions, I had no other explanation for voicing that statement except that the Holy Spirit prompted me. Such a possibility would never have entered my head.

As I contemplated this further, I realized that a meteor is usually just a small pebble or piece of sand speeding through space until it hits our atmosphere and burns up with dramatic effect. The piece of sand I observed had been traveling for perhaps millions of years, yet God determined that at a precise moment in time, to the very second, when one of his children was questioning his love, he directed that piece of sand to enter the atmosphere and burn up. It was a dramatic, visible demonstration of his loving response to my need.

That event was a defining moment. It confirmed for me that God loves me regardless of my performance. I had in a sense issued an ultimatum, a command to God, requesting that he prove himself. That wasn't exactly spiritually mature behavior. But if he would respond to my spontaneous request in such a manner, I could believe he loved me, and that his love was simply for me, without any attendant behaviors, a love for myself alone. It took a while for these truths to become rooted in my heart but eventually they did.

3.

A POUCH OF PRESENCE

Song of Solomon 1:13 *"My Lover is to me a sachet of myrrh resting between my breasts."*

The writer of the Song envisions the Beloved One as carrying a packet of sweet-smelling myrrh between her breasts, as women have for centuries clothed themselves with fragrance. He is speaking of awareness: the mystical presence of Lover to his Beloved, of Beloved to Lover. The metaphor is clear: as the sweet aroma of myrrh, wafting upward from the pouch, caresses her senses she is bathed in the awareness of her Lover. The fragrance engulfs her; thoughts of him consume her. Is he well? Where is he? Is he thinking of me? Does he still love me?

The wafting perfume is an ever-present joy to her. She can't stop thinking about him anymore than she can cut off the flow of sweetness arising up. The picture presents us with one aspect of the nature of love: the intense, incessant preoccupation of a Lover with his Beloved and vice versa. He is always on her mind; she is always on his mind.

11

The Song writer looks beyond the Beloved and Lover. He focuses on the presence of the Lord. The writer does not see God as remote and severe but knows his presence just the way the Beloved knows her Lover. His God is an ever-present reality, an "aroma" never deserting his senses. Whenever the writer's thoughts lift for a moment from his duties, his Heavenly Lover insinuates his way into his awareness. He can no more escape it than can the Beloved escape the aroma drifting up to her nostrils. He welcomes that presence. He glories in it as a supreme delight to him.

Can we sense the writer saying, "How I wish that presence was even more pervasive"? It is a wish that engulfs the earnest lover of Jesus. So many distractions cut off the flow of "aroma". One grieves over the fact that awareness of Jesus' presence is so sketchy, so transient, coming and going. But the intermittent nature of that awareness only creates a more intense longing for the sweetness of his presence. And when we regard ourselves as the Bride of Christ, his Beloved, we discover that Jesus himself initiates the awareness. As the believer opens his or her heart to knowing Jesus more, Jesus fulfills that longing. He is the energy behind his own presence. As the source of a penetrating aroma cannot halt its outward flow, so Jesus does not and will not halt the application of his presence to the loving heart.

May we grasp Jesus' presence more fully, more consistently, more delightfully!

4.

A ROUGH DEFENDER
- Psalm 18:1-19

"I love you, O LORD, my strength. The LORD is my rock and my fortress and my deliverer, my God, my rock, in whom I take refuge, my shield, and the horn of my salvation, my stronghold. I call upon the LORD, who is worthy to be praised, and I am saved from my enemies. The cords of death encompassed me; the torrents of destruction assailed me; the cords of Sheol entangled me; the snares of death confronted me. In my distress I called upon the LORD; to my God I cried for help. From his temple he heard my voice, and my cry to him reached his ears.

Then the earth reeled and rocked; the foundations also of the mountains trembled and quaked, because he was angry. Smoke went up from his nostrils, and devouring fire from his mouth; glowing coals flamed forth from him. He bowed the heavens and came down; thick darkness was under his feet. He rode on a cherub and flew; he came swiftly on the wings of the wind. He made darkness his covering, his canopy around him, thick clouds dark with water. Out of the brightness before him hailstones and coals of fire broke through his clouds.

The LORD also thundered in the heavens, and the Most High uttered his voice, hailstones and coals of fire. And he sent out his arrows and scattered them; he flashed forth lightnings and routed them. Then the channels of the sea were seen, and the foundations of the world were laid bare at your rebuke, O LORD, at the blast of the breath of your nostrils. He sent from on high, he took me; he drew me out of many waters. He rescued me from my strong enemy and from those who hated me, for they were too mighty for me. They confronted me in the day of my calamity, but the LORD was my support. He brought me out into a broad place; he rescued me, because he delighted in me."

King David sat on a Judean hillside, tending his sheep. He watched as a thunderstorm loomed in the distance, gaining power minute by minute, mounting ominously to the sky. It had risen on warm currents of air coming off the Great Sea to the west. The sky blackened. Clouds swirled in all directions. Flashes of lightning darted between the dark formations. The wind stilled, with a sense of pending doom in the quiet air. Not long after he heard the rumble of thunder. It echoed and rolled from one side of the horizon to the other. He saw curtains of rain falling, miles away, as closer and closer the towering clouds approached until they hovered over him, thunder now cracking, booming, even shaking the rocks against which he leans. Lightning threatened to stab David himself. Light fell away as heavy clouds blocked the sun. The earth seemed to reel from the onslaught of the storm, which shook and pounded the ground. Sheets of rain drenched him and pellets of hail beat on his face.

Years later, David recalled that thunderstorm. His life had been tumultuous. That momentous victory over the Philistine giant Goliath soon faded. His life was increasingly threatened by King Saul's jealousy. Saul pursued him through the Judean wildernesses with murderous intent. More years went by and, as the young king of Israel, David found enemy nations surrounding him. They too were intent on destroying him and the nation of Israel. Year after year, leading his mighty army, he marched out against Philistines, Moabites, Ammonites, Edomites, Syrians and more. He defeated them all.

As Psalm 18 opens up, the editor explains why David wrote it: "[He] *addressed the words of this song to the LORD when the LORD rescued him from the hand of all his enemies, and from the hand of Saul."* His mind burst with extravagant praise, describing God in his providential help, metaphor cascading after metaphor: rock, fortress, deliverer, refuge, shield, horn of salvation, stronghold! David was often in situations of mortal danger. He wrote of cords of death, torrents of destruction, cords of Sheol [the grave], snares of death. His natural response was to cry out to God: "*In my distress I called upon the LORD; to my God I cried for help...*" David, ascribing human terms to God, said, "*...and my cry to him reached his ears.*"

What David wrote next, describing God's response, is not just surprising; it is breathtaking, even bewildering. Was he hallucinating? David claimed God was angry with enemies who were trying to destroy him. As we read these fantastic descriptions, one can see David's portrayal of God's anger in violent images. How can he conjure up such extraordinary, fanciful pictures of God? Did God indeed rock the earth? Was smoke pouring from God's nostrils? When did David observe mountains quaking and trembling in God's deliverance of him? Can it really be said of God that he breathed fire, that he thundered in the heavens? When God spared David from Saul's attempts to murder him, did flashes of lightning burst through the clouds surrounding him?

One can almost track David's thinking. David should have been killed many times, by Saul or in warfare by an enemy soldier. Death was an ever-present specter hovering around him. Being mercifully spared, time after time, suddenly loomed in his mind as an awesome, even stupendous act of God. David thought of that thunderstorm long ago. The delivering acts of God were as impressive as the drama of a storm creeping over the pasturelands. David imagined God's efforts on his behalf as the crashing of thunder, flashing of lightning, downpours of rain and hail.

We catch a hint that behind the struggles and dangers David faced, more was going on than the eye could see. If God were involved, it is reasonable to assume there were spiritual dynamics at play. David's earthly enemies may well have been driven unwittingly by spiritual forces who had a desire to thwart God's plan for this special king of Israel. David seemed to have had an inkling that the fierce battles between these spiritual forces "in heavenly places" were behind the assaults against him.

And is it unreasonable to think our deliverance from sin also entails powerful forces that oppose God's salvation plan for us? The apostle Paul spoke of Christ's followers *"wrestling, not against flesh and blood but against the rulers, against the authorities, against the cosmic powers over this present darkness, against the spiritual forces of evil in the heavenly places"* (Eph 6:12). In Paul's prayer for the Ephesians, he prayed that believers would have new spiritual enlightenment concerning God's incredible power *"toward you"* (1:19). He wrote that it was equivalent to the power God exercised in raising Christ from the dead. That is, *"exceedingly great"* power on God's part was necessary to accomplish our salvation. Paul prayed that we may become more and more aware of the spiritual conflicts that took place in heavenly places before we could become children of God.

Because David imagined cosmic forces involved in the deliverance he experienced, it prompted him to begin his psalm with an amazing statement, found nowhere else in Scripture: *"I love you, O LORD."* The more we are aware of the power of God in choosing and protecting us, the easier it will be for us to say, "I love you, O Lord!"

5.
A SUMMER MORN

How savory is a summer morn,
A freshness, as the day is born;
Enough to cure a soul forlorn.
Work? Play? How one's torn!

Our star reigns higher every hour.
Fair light exerts its welcome power,
Splashing rays on grass and flower,
Gracing all with radiant shower.

6.
A TALKING GOD – Psalm 19:1-6

"The heavens declare the glory of God, and the sky above proclaims his handiwork.

Day to day pours out speech, and night to night reveals knowledge.

There is no speech, nor are there words, whose voice is not heard.

Their voice goes out through all the earth, and their words to the end of the world. In them [the heavens] he has set a tent for the sun,

which comes out like a bridegroom leaving his chamber, and, like a strong man, runs its course with joy.

Its rising is from the end of the heavens, and its circuit to the end of them, and there is nothing hidden from its heat."

Psalm 19 is a masterpiece of creative writing. David the Psalmist was so adept at metaphor and word-pictures. Who taught him how to write? Where did he get such insights? Was his talent merely the Holy Spirit "imposing" words and sentences on him, or did David possess this talent inherently? Of course, in reality, God gives such abilities but if the Spirit were not inspiring David's words, would he, David, still have written so poetically and profoundly?

The psalm opens with a declaration: *"The heavens are broadcasting the glory of God."* The term "glory" suggests "that which is lofty", the sky as the visible universe. It is plain that David was an observer of the heavens. Did the fascination with the heavens come to him while he sat out on a Judean hillside as a young shepherd? Through the long dark hours of the night the stars would shine with brilliance in the cool dry air of the sheep lands. The cloud-like mass of our galaxy center would rotate through the arc of the sky. He would note movements of prominent star-planets, wondering why they seemed to stray. Did David puzzle over the moon's faithful cycle? How its face was altered with each passing night, rising later and later, changing from round to crescent, and a few days later reversing its profile from crescent to full circle again? Did meteors intrigue him, those unpredictable streaks of light flashing across the sky, some dim, some blazing like fire?

To David, these phenomena were revelatory. They communicated a message. Like almost everyone else around him, he could have dismissed it all with some mythological explanations. Folklore about the moon, sun and stars prevailed; they were worshiped by non-Israelite peoples. But David believed firmly that this sky above him was declaring truth: a profound message about God and from God. God was communicating his glory, by night and by day.

What would David mean by the "glory of God"? The Hebrew word for glory, *"kabod"*, literally meant "weight", something pressing down, making an impression. So, David was saying that God's nature, his being, shone through the wonders of the sky, making a huge impression. There was nothing feeble in this communication of God's glory. It was unmistakably weighty. God intended for his creative glory to be seen in such a way that no one could miss it. All that David could see, he attributed to the work of God. God's "hands" produced all David observed. David could only make this statement out of a conviction that his God, the LORD, Yahweh, was the Creator of all things.

This communication of God's glory was constant. By day, every day, the works of God *"pour out knowledge"*. Even the nights, especially the nights, revealed this incredible knowledge of this Creator God. This God had created all that David could see around and above him.

One example of God's glory became a metaphoric picture in David's mind. The sun, blazing across the sky, was like a proud bridegroom bursting out of his room, boldly ready to take on the challenge of marriage and family. Like the bridegroom, the sun *"runs its course with joy"*. Or, in another picture, it's like a *"strong man"*, maybe a warrior, plunging into battle with confidence. Nothing can outdo the sun. Its radiant light and heat permeate the earth. It is impressive. One cannot even gaze at it in its full splendor. But it was only a weak representation of the impressive image of the radiant glory of God. And to David's mind, this message was universal. Just as the sun's heat blanketed the earth, so this message of God's glory is never limited. All people can hear this message, if only they have ears to hear.

In a fascinating insight David said there was no real speech or language with this communication. No audible voice can be heard. Yet unmistakably something is being said. Years ago, Francis Schaeffer, Christian writer and teacher, wrote a book titled "He is There and He is not Silent". It's what David discovered so many centuries ago. What he learned contradicts the two lies the world generally presents: God doesn't count and he has nothing to say.

After the question of what is being said, a follow-up question is: how does one apprehend what is spoken? And then, who is listening?

Perhaps the apostle Paul had David's words in mind when he wrote in Romans 1:19-20: *"For what can be known about God is plain to them, because God has shown it to them. For his invisible attributes, namely, his eternal power and divine nature, have been clearly perceived, ever since the creation of the world, in the things that have been made. So they are without excuse."* In line with David's thoughts, Paul insisted that God's *"eternal power and divine nature"* can be seen in what has been created. And it is grasped by faith in God. The message of Romans 1 is a sad one. The world generally rejected the truth, not worshiping the God of Creation but making for themselves other objects of worship.

But for those who embrace the truth David gives us, every time we turn our face to the heavens, we can rejoice in the greatness of God. And as we feel the warmth of the sun bathe our face, we can give thanks to God for revealing his glory.

"I will say to the Lord,
My refuge and my fortress,
my God, in whom I trust."
(Psalm 91:2)

7.
AFRAID OF FLYING

I sat in the coffee shop, gazing out a window. I spot a small flock of geese – just 5 of them – as they glide over the meadow nearby. Wings extended, no flapping, feet dropping like a plane's landing gear. They turn and bank as one, descending slowly, orderly. Some patch of land, or maybe a pond, was their target.

I thought as they drifted lower and lower, what must it look like from heights above the earth? "Bird's eye view" is a phrase we use but don't actually experience, unless in a plane or hang gliding. Even then we can't experience it like a bird would. We're just strapped into a seat in an aluminum tube at the mercy of others who control all aspects of the flight.

I wondered if birds ever get scared, afraid of falling. They don't look as if they are ever fearful. They seem so confident in their flying. They should be afraid because all else that goes up in the air falls to the ground. But birds have learned how to overcome the pull of gravity. There they are – soaring, swooping, gliding, darting, ascending, descending – all without falling. They are not afraid.

In their fledging nesting days, fear gripped them, but only briefly. Very early, out of the nest, they learned they could fly! Did they, in their little bird brains, marvel at that? Probably not. They just do it. It was instinctive. They fly as naturally as can be.

Someone once posted in Facebook that the phrase, "Do not be afraid" appears in Scripture 365 times, one instance for every day of the year. A nice "coincidence"! As a believer in Christ, I am learning to "fly" through life, without being afraid of falling or failing. Learning to soar, glide, dart, twist, turn – all naturally and without fear. The existing spiritual forces of the world are against me, pulling, pulling me down. But I learn, in the Spirit, that I have faculties, resources, to counteract those forces. I have "wings". I can fly. The prophet Isaiah uses the metaphor of flying to assure God's saints that they can overcome the pull of the fallen world: *"Those who wait in trust on the Lord shall mount up with wings like eagles..."* Isaiah 40:31). Fear of falling has been left far behind. The grasp the earth has on me has been broken. *"Walk in the Spirit and you will not succumb to the downward pull of the flesh,"* says the apostle Paul (Galatians 5:16). *"Trust in the Lord with all your heart..."* says the writer of Proverbs, and the Lord will direct your way (Proverbs 3:5-6). You will not crash in the meadows of life.

What a gift – to be able to fly!

8.
AMEN! AMEN!

Psalm 41 closes with *"Amen! Amen!"* It's David the Psalmist's first "Amen" in a Psalm, and maybe his only one. Three other instances of a double "Amen" occur in Psalms: in 72:19 (from Solomon), 89:52 and 106:48 (from Ethan), where people are exhorted to say "Amen! Amen".

The word in Hebrew is pronounced "ah-<u>mane</u>", just as some pronounce it in English, although others pronounce it "ay-men". It's meaning is "truly", or "so be it", a term indicating strong affirmation, a declaration saying "This is it!". When used in repetition, the emphasis is heightened. Greater stress is put on what is declared to be.

Another biblical reference to a double Amen is in Nehemiah 8:6. An assembly of Israelites had asked Ezra the scribe to read the "Book of Moses". As he opened the scroll, praised God, and read aloud. Then people lifted their hands and cried, "Amen! Amen!", as they bowed their heads and worshiped the Lord. The hearing of God's Word had such a profound effect on them that they punctuated the occasion with not just one but two "Amens"!

It is very interesting that the Greek word "αμην" comes through exactly as the Hebrew word for Amen. It is translated as "Amen" 29 times in the New Testament. But when the English translation "truly" or "verily" is added, the number becomes more than 152. Most are in statements by Jesus, but Paul often emphasizes a strong declaration with "Amen!" He closes all his letters with Amen, as do other writers. When Jesus uses it in John's Gospel, it is always a double "Amen".

Both Greek and Hebrew needed an expression that would signify a declaration as being authentic and of great importance. It was weighty. Attention should be paid to it. When Jesus prefaced a statement in the Gospels with "Amen", it was equivalent to *"He who has ears to hear, let him hear."* Perhaps "Listen up!" comes closest in English when a speaker wants his hearers to pay attention. Or "That's it!" when a fact is stated.

It's of interest that the last word in our Bible is "Amen"! (Revelation 22:21), as if the Holy Spirit was saying, "This is it! The whole truth of God! The entire story of salvation!"

Thus, the use of "Amen" signifies an inescapable fact that some truths must be emphasized because of the great significance attached to them. When Jesus said "Amen, Amen", what he had to say had spiritual life and death implications. Our inveterate lack of focus creates the need for that kind of emphasis. Our attention drifts easily from serious realities we can't see to the mundane which is in front of us.

We have retained the use of "Amen" in our current language, especially for Christians, in a couple of ways. When moved by a statement of truth or excited by an event, we exclaim, "Amen!" In certain church traditions, when a statement by the preacher resonates strongly with the congregation, it's expected that a chorus of "Amens" would punctuate the air. Whether in church or in individual declarations, we somewhat naturally apply "Amen" in the way it was meant to be used. It becomes an affirmation of the importance of what we read, hear or experience.

Our most frequent use of "Amen" is to end our prayers. The practice originated most likely because some manuscripts of the New Testament close the Lord's Prayer with "Amen". As time went on, it was assumed that all prayers should close with an affirmative "Amen". But when we attach it to the end of a prayer, it seems to get trivialized, like a ritualized sign-off to God. It rarely carries the true meaning of "Amen", rendering the real meaning of "Amen" empty.

That real meaning of "Amen" calls us to use it with great intention. If we end our prayer with "Amen", we should say it emphatically. As we reflect on the substance of our prayer, an "Amen" indicates the earnestness with which we approach God.

And when we are moved by some event, some word of preaching, some blessing from God – we can accentuate it with a hearty "Amen!', audibly or silently. Focusing on "Amen's" true meaning lends weightiness to every such experience.

9.

An Old Apostle's Christmas

(based on 1 John 1:1-3)

The old apostle writes, hunched over his table,
casting a backward glance in time.
He warms to his theme,
a theme never far from heart and mind –
"We knew Him!"
He has written it before.
Countless times more has he spoken of it,
always with deep joy flooding his heart.
Once again the thrill rises, leaving his eyes misty:
We saw Him!
How dull were our eyes at the start!
Just another man,
Israelite, young, ordinary yet so unusual,
grimy feet, sweaty face.
He sighed, he cried.
He shivered, he napped.
Dusty robe, aching back.
He laughed, he scolded.
Touched lepers, stopped winds, opened eyes, ears.
Questions lay unasked within us:
"Who was He?"
Years passed before we knew, before light dawned –
We had heard Him!

We had seen Him!
We had touched Him!
GOD!

The twelve of us! We lived with God, and didn't know it!
"That which was from the beginning!"
He lived with us.
God had His arm around me! Me!
What honor and glory!
I can still feel that touch.
God touched me!

"No man has ever seen God."
We knew that, but, but. . .
We _did_ see Him.
He looked at me with God's eyes.
At me!
A privilege past understanding!

I heard the very voice of God!
God spoke to me,
and my ears still ring with those words!
God's words. The real God's real words!
To me!

'The Life was made manifest...the Eternal Life which was with
the Father..."
That was God with us, truly God.
We saw God! We touched God! We heard God!

The old Apostle straightens himself, rejoicing in such a
marvelous experience!

10.
CAUSE OR ALLOW?

Terrorists fly two planes into the World Trade Center towers in New York, killing thousands. A devastating storm ravishes the coast of Texas. The same in Florida. A deranged man shoots up a school, murdering 20 children and six adults. A 2004 tsunami off the coast of Indonesia kills over 250,000 people. Jamison and Kathryne Pals and their three children, committed to mission work, and heading to Colorado for final training, are all killed on a Nebraska interstate. A semitrailer truck rear-ended their minivan in 2016. An embittered man enters a church in Texas and slaughters more than 20 people. A young mother dies of cancer, leaving a husband and 3 small children to grieve her death.

Stories of tragedy, calamity and suffering abound. We wrestle with these events as they grip our hearts, and inevitably we raise serious questions about God's involvement. Two questions frequently come to the fore: did God cause these events, or did God simply allow them to happen? There are serious problems with each question.

Did God cause the tragedy, the accident, the illness? If we think in these terms, we turn God into an agent of suffering and even of evil. It flies in the face of the biblical picture of God as kind and good and loving. And also of much Scripture such as Psalm 91 which proclaims God's providential care. If God causes the calamity, he presents himself as a hurtful God. We naturally shy away from referring to God as the cause of pain and suffering.

If we reject the "God caused it" scenario, then we tend to say he allowed the accident or tragedy to come about, thus avoiding the dilemma of a loving God creating a hurtful situation. God's reputation for goodness and kindness remains intact. Countless books have been written on this subject, trying to get God "off the hook", so to speak. Christians easily quote Romans 8:28, claiming that God works in all these difficult situations, bringing good out of them for *"those who love God"*. That, we suppose, redeems the tragedy. But to claim that God simply allows something to happen leaves us with a God who appears somewhat helpless in the face of evil and suffering. He may not cause it, we say, but once it happens, all he can do is work his healing hand to salvage something good from an unfortunate situation.

Can we then conclude that there are mighty forces wreaking havoc on the earth that God has no control over? Has he withdrawn some of his restraining power, allowing evil forces to afflict our world? It appears from the opening lines of the book of Job that God "allows" suffering and calamity to take place. Satan approached God pointing out that Job's faith in God was only because of the benefit he got out of it – God's blessings and favor. The drama unfolds with God "allowing" Satan to afflict Job severely, with the loss of family, health and wealth.

The "God allows" approach is fraught with problems. The question arises: if God allows other powers to inflict harm, can he not also disallow them too? He could have restrained Satan from acting against Job. It seemed as if it was within his control. And if God allowed the calamity to happen, how does that not involve him somehow in causation?

How do we resolve the "allow/cause" dilemma, an issue that has plagued theologians and Christian thinkers for centuries. Many books have been written attempting to exonerate God, trying to defend his honor. It is remarkable that Scripture itself does not attempt to defend God in terms of evil, pain and suffering. The exception to that is the book of Job which is a brilliant piece of writing.

In the Job drama, his friends accused him of gross hidden sin. Hence his suffering. But Job protested, rejecting their judgmental conclusions. Instead, he accused God of treating him unfairly. He, Job, had done nothing wrong. To Job, God has indeed <u>caused</u> all this misfortune though he cannot understand why. God appeared to be set against him for some mysterious reason. Job spoke endlessly of his innocence and of God's reluctance to recognize that.

In Job 13:15, he was convinced God was so against him that he stated, *"He will surely slay me; I have no hope; yet I will defend my ways before his face."*

Job's friends tried to justify God. To them God was only doing what his nature demanded: punish a sinful man. Job rejected their claims and attempted to justify himself.

In the end, Job was exhausted; he could say no more. At that point God spoke out of a whirlwind. He peppered Job with question after question, all about the created order: "Where were you, Job, when...?" "Can you understand how...?" "Can you explain this...?" All the questions forced Job to conclude that he knew almost nothing. It appeared that God was essentially telling Job: "You accuse me of causing the calamity that has befallen you, all the time protesting your innocence. But, Job, you can't even explain the mysteries of the natural world. How then can you begin to understand what is going on in the realm of the spiritual world? The dynamics of good and evil? Or can you explain how spiritual beings interact with and impact individuals like yourself? There is far more involved with these events than you can address by accusing me of 'causing' them. Or, if it would be known to you, that I 'allowed' your suffering. As you do not have the intellectual ability to understand most processes in the natural realm, much less do you have the capacity to explain the calamities which have come upon you."

It seems we must come to a similar conclusion. The words "allow" or "cause" are totally inadequate to explain what is really going on in the realm of calamity and suffering, good and evil. Human language has limited ability to convey these spiritual realities. And the witness of Scripture is that the human mind cannot grasp the ways of God:

Isaiah 55:8-9 – *"For my thoughts are not your thoughts, neither are your ways my ways, declares the LORD. For as the heavens are higher than the earth, so are my ways higher than your ways and my thoughts than your thoughts."*

Romans 11:33-34 – *"Oh, the depth of the riches and wisdom and knowledge of God! How unsearchable are his judgments and how inscrutable his ways! For who has known the mind of the Lord, or who has been his counselor?"*

Psalm 145:3 – *"Great is the LORD, and greatly to be praised, and his greatness is unsearchable."*

God's ways and God's thoughts have an unfathomable nature to them. And in the end, we must trust God to accomplish his loving purposes, even in the face of evil and suffering. Something even Job had to do.

11.

CLEOME

I was thinking about cleomes. My cleomes! Well, not really mine! They belong to God! And the angel in charge of cleomes! They are a flower that graces our yard with uncommon beauty and glory. They were there last year, and the year before, and a few years before that. I planted them in one of those years, and then I left them alone. Turns out, they didn't need me. "We can handle ourselves quite nicely, thank you very much, Mr. Johnson." They kept coming back, thrusting their stalks into the air, up to 5 or 6 feet. All summer, without my help or attention, they radiate their peculiar glory. They are unique, like no other flower.

In fact, all flowers are unique, so creatively distinct from all others. In the fall, when the cleome have had enough of hot weather, they get together somehow and decide how they will keep this glory thing going. Ingenious, the plan they came up with! Each stalk would develop pods and in each pod they would deposit dozens of seeds. And each seed would be imbued with cleome-life. Each plant then descended into nether regions of the earth never to be seen again. But before it departed eternally, its pods dry up, and then one day, Pop!, they burst open and strew the seeds all over, extravagantly. Seed by seed sank into the uncaring soil, there to endure long months of bitter cold.

Excitedly, every May, I trudge out to my cleome patch in the back yard. Did they survive? Where are they? Those little green heads poking out of the ground? Aaahh, yes! My cleome! The cleome-angel has faithfully brought them through. Week by week they take on their special cleome character. Amazingly, they do it all over again. I watch, but I can do nothing. They were an inch tall, now 2 weeks later they are up to 4". They vie with each other for space to display their beauty, so I have to thin them out. Each one I pluck out had hoped to be a reflector of God's glory, but nobly sacrifices its life for the others. Week by week, they climb again into dizzying height. They burst into blossom, petals clustered together. They sway in the wind, bowing and tossing to accentuate their beauty. They don't need me. I give them nothing. But unasked they give me so much, and ask nothing in return.

How can one not marvel at that and praise the God of cleome?

12.

SIN AGAINST LOVE

I sinned against love,
the worst kind of sin.
Angels shudder, stand aghast,
Stunned to behold,
Powerless to grasp:
"How can one sin against love?"
So unnatural, so blind, so heartless!
Only madness sins against such wealth of love.

I sinned against love,
the only kind of sin.
All acts lead to him "with whom we have to do".
"Against thee,
thee only,
have I sinned."
A sin against him who so loved the world
that he gave,
gave his only son,
gave to save from sin.

I sinned against love,
the best kind of sin.
Angels watch with eager hope,
knowing atonement's great work.
Forgiveness – a confession away!

Only love forgives!
Only love remembers no more!
Only love heals sin's fatal wounds.
He who declares his sin
is immersed in the
agape love
of God!

13.

CLINGING

David said to God, *"My soul clings to You..."* (Psalm 63:8). He began the Psalm expressing how desperately he thirsted for God. Now he turned his thoughts in verse 8 to another desperation word: "cling". It translates the Hebrew word *dawbak*. One Hebrew concordance piles on synonym after synonym: *"cling, stay close, cleave to, keep close, stick with...."* The Message Bible says, *"I hold on to you for dear life."* There is little doubt of the intensity of David's clinging to God. David's hunger for God, his intimate attachment to God, captivates us.

But David is not so enamored of his own clinging to God. The verse goes on to suggest he recognizes he could not begin to thirst after God, praise or bless him, or even cling to him, unless this were true: *"Your right hand upholds me,"* or more accurately, *"...hangs on to me"*. Again, The Message Bible: *"You hold me steady as a rock."* As certainly as "cling to" may correspond to the NT "believe in", the "upholds me" presents us with the New Testament concept of "grace". The message of the Scriptures is not focused on our clinging to God. The focus is rather on the God who holds on to us. The truth arise out of the steadfast love of God –*"chesed"*, spoken of in verse 3. This was New Testament grace poured out on David, a follower of God who knew more of what life with God involved than do most modern Christians.

The old poet George Herbert of the 1600's wrote of Christ as a "Holdfast". His thought supports the idea that it is God who holds us, who in fact initiates the connection we have with him. Herbert expressed that, though he himself strove to keep the ways of God, it was not in his ability to do so. Only by what he had been given by Christ was he able to cling to God.

"I threatened to observe the strict decree
Of my dear God with all my power and might.
But I was told by one, it could not be;
Yet I might trust in God to be my light.

Then will I trust, said I, in him alone.
Nay, even to trust in him, was also his:
We must confess that nothing is our own.
Then I confess that he my only help is:

But to have nothing is ours, not to confess
That we have nothing. I stood amazed at this,
Much troubled, till I heard a friend express,
That all things were more ours by being his.
What Adam had, and forfeited for all,
Christ keeps now, who cannot fail or fall."

The holding power of God on me is immeasurably greater and stronger than my clinging grasp on him.

14.
DELIGHTS

The grumble, rumble of thunder
Or its blast in the ear,
Or the roof pit-pat of rain,
Are noises held dear.

They may call us to dance,
These clouds that we love;
Always remember,
They're a gift from above.

That moon circles softly,
That ball we adore.
It points to God's grace,
Ours evermore.
Of flowers, rocks, and horses
And shore lines of sand,
Let's never forget,
They come from God's hand.

Can we be friends?

15.

DIRECTIONS – Psalm 89:12

In Psalm 89 the Psalmist Ethan the Ezrahite wrote of the power and love that God gave to David. He exalted God as Creator, over and over. Then he made a strange statement to God: *"You created the north and the south"* (vs. 12). What a grand insight! It strikes me as an unusual observation that a person would hardly think of: the directions of the compass were created by God. And making use of earthly directions - north, south, east, west - is a gift from God. How wonderful to have directions! It's a unique thought, that God has given us directions in order to guide our lives. Instead of a chaotic here or there, we can know which way is which, and some people know that better than others! How good of God to help us structure life in this way!

Instinctively, we know it is important to be aware of which way we are moving. I read of a 66 year old Tennessee woman, Geraldine Largay, who died in 2013 while walking the Appalachian Trail. She and a companion had been on the trail, off and on, for a number of months, having completed 1000 miles. However, when her companion left, Geraldine kept on, but got lost in Maine. She was only two miles off the trail but was not found for 26 months. She was thought to know something about hiking, but others reported of her that she lacked a sense of direction, and may not have even known how to use a compass.

Without directions, we are truly lost. We don't know which way to set out or where we will end up. This way? That way? How can we know? Not having a firm grasp on direction creates great anxiety. For direction to function, we must have signs that tell us which way is which. The whole world operates, both intuitively and explicitly, on a foundation of direction. Where the sun rises is always east. Where it sets is always west. And about noon the sun tends toward the south. Early on in human experience it was found that a certain prominent star - Polaris, or the North Star – always remained fixed in the north.

Along with his gift of direction, God gave humanity the intelligence needed to discern direction. Humans learned how to use directional tools such as landmarks to provide navigation: rocks, hills, streams, trees. Early travelers looked for these to assure them of the right direction. Later, explorers the world over, inordinately brave, rendered a tremendous service by creating maps, at first crude drawings, later refined more and more. Along with maps, God provided other technology to assist with direction.

The reality of physical direction may serve as a metaphor for "life direction". Even while we are physically moving east or west, north or south, everyone's life is moving in a certain direction as well. To what end or purpose are we here? How can we know whether the direction of our lives is consistent with those ends? The coordinates are of course different, and the ability to determine what direction one is moving may be complicated. If we have a God who gave us the ability to navigate on the earth, might he not also have provided directions for life as well? And the means for discerning whether the direction we take is helpful or harmful?

An old proverb says, "If we do not change direction, we will arrive at where we are going." A loving God wants to give our lives direction. The Psalmist David asked of God, *"Show me your ways, O Lord, teach me your paths"* (Psalm 25:4).

That's an appeal to know direction. Just a few verses later David said, *"Good and upright is the Lord; therefore, he instructs sinners in the way"* (verse 8). And a few Psalms later he wrote of God saying, *"I will instruct you and teach you the way you should go..."* (32:8).

Jesus understood the idea of spiritual direction. In his final meeting with his disciples, he announced that he was going away and that the disciples knew where he was going. But one disciple, Thomas, burst out, *"Lord, we don't know where you are going. How can we know the way?"* (14:5). Jesus' response was not really an answer to Thomas' question, but a significant word about following a certain direction: "I *am* the Way, *the Truth and the Life. No one comes to the Father except through me"* (John 14:6). Thomas was thinking more in the physical realm of direction. Jesus pronounced himself as the one who would provide ultimate direction for life itself, a spiritual direction.

Thus, Jesus assumed the role that God first promised through David: *"I will teach you the way..."* To anyone who asks, "What direction shall I go in life?", Jesus says, "Come with me. I am your direction and way and life."

16.

DO YOU LOVE ME?

John 21:15-22

1. He fed us on that sandy beach,
   Fish and bread, freshly baked;
   His presence there a sudden treat.
   Why was he beside our lake?

2. Like a shame-faced guilty child
   I stood before him fearful, nervous,
   Thinking of all my flaws piled high,
   Still a disciple fit for service?

3. With arm draped round me easily,
   He quietly led me some ways apart.

Here it comes – he would dismiss me!
I moved along with sinking heart.

4. He asked the question graciously,
   Addressing me by special name:
   "Peter, do you love just me?
   More than fish, or John or James?"

5. "Lord, you know you mean so much to me.
   You've held my heart right from day one."
   "Feed my lambs," he said surprisingly.
   Does he mean my work's not done?

6. "Do you love me, Peter?", a second time.
   "Lord, I count you very dear."
   Is he just toying with my mind?
   "Tend my sheep!" did I just hear?

'7. The third time was a heavy blow:
   "Am I really so special to you?"
   Grieving in heart, I whispered low,
   "Lord, you know what's true."

8. Agape love I could not claim;
   Three denials proved that true.
   "Tend my sheep" – his charge the same,
   "I have work for you to do."

9. Friend John was now approaching us.
   I quickly asked "What of him?"
   "Don't fret. Make me your focus."
   Then "Follow Me!" – that call again.

10. "My disciple, beloved child,
Love me most, even more than any?"
"Lord so precious, who for me died,
May love for you surpass the many."

17.
EVEN SO COME –
Revelation 22:20

They sang with quiet passion. They sang wistfully. They sang with yearning: "Lord Jesus, come. Even so, come. We wait for you." That message by the worship team pulled at the congregation, voicing a theme often neglected. The imagery is compelling: "Every heart longing for our King...like a bride waiting for her groom".

In listening we are drawn to the second last verse in Revelation, actually the last word from John the Apostle before his sign-off, the last of Jesus' words to his church: *"Amen! Come, Lord Jesus!"* John spoke for his church. He echoed the longing she had felt over many years of harassment by a world hostile to Jesus Christ.

The concept of Jesus' coming back moves on two tracks. The first is a promise: Jesus himself promised he would return. Significantly, it was John who most explicitly wrote of that promise. In an upper room where he and the disciples ate a last Passover meal before his arrest, Jesus took the opportunity to teach at length, with some concluding and ultimate truths. He offered a new commandment: *"love one another"*. He introduced the Holy Spirit as a new Teacher-Helper who would dwell within the disciples. But most shockingly, he told them he was going away, going away to prepare a place for them. They would not see him anymore nor have him as their Teacher. But before the disciples could voice any protest, Jesus assured them that he would come back: *"...if I go and prepare a place for you, I will come again..."*

(John 14:3). A few moments later, he reiterated his promise, *"I will come to you"* (14:18).

Immediately after, Jesus and the disciples walked to Gethsemane, where in the darkness hostile foes arrested him. He then suffered brutal treatment by his enemies, and the agony he endured as he bore mankind's sins and surrendered to death. Was that his predicted going away? He was laid in a tomb and then resurrected. Was that Jesus' coming back again? But it was not to be.

Not many days after Jesus' resurrection he led a large host of disciples to the Mount of Olives. While they watched, he blessed them and quickly vanished from their sight. Another going away! The assembled crowd stood gaping until two angels appeared and said, *"Why are you staring at the sky? This Jesus, whom you saw taken up into heaven, will come back again..."* (Acts 1:11)

The second track regarding Jesus' promise is the response of his follow-ers. The thought of his return captured the heart of the early church. While the first apostles fully believed the promise, it was Paul who over and over kept it alive to the early believers. In every letter, he referenced the excit-ing promise Jesus made: *I will come again*. There was no doubt in his mind that Jesus' coming would be very soon, probably in Paul's lifetime. The time was indeed short and there was a lot of territory to cover with the gospel message. Excitement and the joyful anticipation of seeing Jesus filled their hearts.

Long decades passed. No Jesus appeared. Gradually Paul's letters seemed to lack the same urgency as previously. His first letter, 1 Thessalonians, drips with anticipation of Jesus' return. His last letter, 2 Timothy, features a single glancing reference in which Paul appears to say he will be martyred before that wonderful event occurred.

It was John who renewed the promise. His Lord had not returned during John's long life. Was the promise no longer valid? Why had Jesus delayed his return? Suddenly, on the island called Patmos, John's world exploded and disillusionment vanished. In the Spirit, a fantastic vision of the glorious Jesus captivated his soul. Jesus, in dramatic symbolism, portrayed for John the world events and spiritual conflicts that would precede his return for his church, before his people were ushered into an eternal realm.

As the full picture of God's eternal plan came to a conclusion, John heard Jesus speak again, *"Behold, I am coming soon"* (Rev 22:12). It was an echo of what had first been spoken many years before on that momentous night before the awful arrest in Gethsemane: *"I am going away"*, and then the promise, *"I will come again."* In John's vision, Jesus reiterated that promise, this time emphatically, *"Yes, for sure, I am coming soon"* (vs. 20). And then John voiced what Jesus' church feels so deeply: *"Amen! Come for sure, Lord Jesus!"* His statement carried exactly the same emphatic word Jesus used, "Yes indeed, I'm coming soon", "Yes indeed, Lord Jesus, come!!"

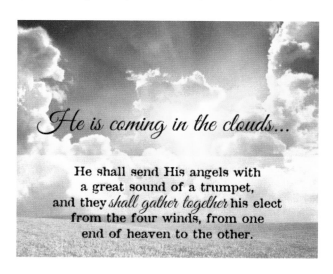

He is coming in the clouds...

He shall send His angels with
a great sound of a trumpet,
and they *shall gather together* his elect
from the four winds, from one
end of heaven to the other.

It was a word of deep longing, of great yearning. Having come to know Jesus in spirit through the word of the apostles, the church had become heart-bound to Jesus. They wanted him. And he wanted them.

Centuries passed. The church experienced battering, it drifted, was persecuted, endured heretical teaching and much more. Yet the Enemy has not been able to eradicate a longing for the return of Jesus. The desire has ebbed and flowed but among those who are faithful to Jesus, it burns bright. True believers in Jesus feed their souls on this promise, *"For sure, I am coming soon."* The more Jesus' church meditates on this promise, the more their yearning hearts respond, *"Amen! For sure come, Lord Jesus."*

"It is good to give thanks to the Lord... and to declare his steadfast love in the morning, and his faithfulness at night." (Psalm 92:1-2)

18.

FIVE PEOPLE I WANT TO MEET IN HEAVEN

In 2003 Mitch Albom wrote a book titled "The Five People You Meet in Heaven." The title came to mind as I thought of some persons from my past.

We may wonder about those who have gone before us. Where are they and what are they experiencing? However, for those who have not yet passed away, we pray they may go to be with Christ when they too sleep the sleep of death.

In my imagination, I envision meeting in heaven with certain people who have entered my circle of life in the past. I would like to ask them some questions, discover some hidden truths about their lives.

LEONARD NICOTINE –

Red Pheasant Indian Reserve, populated by a tribe of Cree natives, lies about 25 miles south of North Battleford, Saskatchewan, Canada. Many years ago, my father out of a passion to share the gospel of Jesus Christ with native Canadians, traveled weekly to Red Pheasant. Resistance was strong, so persuading natives to believe in Jesus was difficult. Those few who did come to faith in Christ were harassed for their stand. One of the first to embrace Christianity was Leonard Nicotine. Life as a Christian was very difficult for him. He was taunted and persecuted, and his children were ill-treated at the Catholic residential school.

As a young teen, I would drive out to the reserve with my father. We had a Ford pickup truck with an enclosed box built on the back. I often drove around the reserve, on mostly dirt and sometimes muddy roads, picking up Christian natives. They would gather at one of the homes. The homes were very primitive, with few amenities.

Fast forward to 2006. My father passed away at age 87. At my dad's funeral, a young lady approached me as I stood by my dad's casket. She was Leonard Nicotine's daughter Patty. She told me this story: Leonard and his wife had remained faithful to Christ. One Thanksgiving the family was gathered around the table to eat. Leonard told his wife and 12 children that all they had to eat for Thanksgiving meal was a rabbit that Leonard had snared that morning. His wife had boiled up the meat, and now they sat down at the table. Leonard, with tears in his eyes, said, "We will give thanks to God for the rabbit we have." When he had finished praying, there was a knock on the door. When the door was opened, there was my father and his sidekick Jack Newsham. They had bags of groceries, including a turkey for their meal. Patty said to me, "I became a Christian because of that experience." She went on to tell me that they were part of a house church movement among natives. The year before they had baptized 50 people.

I want to ask Leonard how he came to faith in Christ and how he had stayed faithful to him all those difficult years. I'd like to know what difficulties he experienced in walking with Christ in a hostile environment, and how he shepherded his children to faith in Christ.

ARVID ELVES –

I was 7 years old. My father, fresh out of a seminary in Saskatoon, Saskatchewan, Canada, took a pastoral position at Torch River, Saskatchewan. It was a desolate place for him and his family of three children. Literally, roads ended two miles north of our house. And it was a poor excuse for a house. An unpainted wood frame structure, wood floors, full of dust, in some disrepair. Facilities were outside. It was not unknown for rats to show their faces at times. The church building stood across a barely recognizable parking lot. In the dark of night, I could hear coyotes yipping and wolves howling in the fields next to the house. With the light of a full moon, I could look out the window and see them running around the field. Going outside to use the outhouse during the night was a terrifying experience. Bear droppings could be spotted along our path in nearby woods.

The congregation was small, made up mostly of families working marginal farms, struggling to raise crops in such a far north climate. In this mix was Arvid Elves, a young man who lived a few miles from the church. Faithfully every Sunday he came to church on his own. He was a common man, without pretensions. I recall his ebullient spirit. Though the circumstances of his life were modest, he had a happy approach to everything.

The rigors of Arvid's life were symbolized by what I heard of his travels to and from church. He rode his bike, through all kinds of weather, over basically muddy rutted dirt roads. Arvid related some of the adventures he experienced on the way to church. Once, having encountered a huge timber wolf on the road, he dismounted his bike and walked slowly around and away from the wolf. That happened more than once. At another time, a large bear blocked his way. Again, he had to slowly walk his way past this predator.

Yet Arvid stayed faithful to Jesus Christ. Many years later, when my father took a church in North Battleford, Arvid would frequently visit us. He loved my mother and father. They had accepted him for who he was.

I want to ask Arvid how he came to faith in Christ, and what continued to drive him in a faithful journey with Jesus. I would want to know more of what he thought of as he biked to church.

Leonard Nicotine and Arvid Elves have moved on into the presence of the Lord. The next three persons are still alive. And I am not totally certain of their spiritual status.

MARTINA –

It was in September of 2006. Wanting an adventure, to travel just on my own, I set off in our Honda van. I headed west and south, eventually ending up at the North Rim of the Grand Canyon. At 8000' above sea level, there was a pronounced chill in the air in mid-September. I found a campground and settled in for a couple of days.

The second night brought a young couple next to me. I found out they were Peter and Martina, Czechoslovakians from Maryland. We visited a bit before I went to my van to sleep. The next morning, I saw Peter and Martina packing up to leave. I felt compelled to go over to talk with them. I approached Martina and said, "God has shown me that he loves me, and loves you too." She seemed rather startled, as if this had never occurred to her. Immediately, she responded, "How do you know that?" I said I had to experience it for myself. Again, she asked, "How did that happen?" I told her that I had been desperate at one point and cried out to God to show me whether he loved me or not, and he had made it clear that he did. I then asked her if I could pray for her. She asked, "Right now?" I said "Yes." I prayed for Martina, that God would prove to her that he loved her. Then I said to her, "When you think about God, say to him that you want to know him better. And keep saying it to him." She seemed definitely intrigued, and a bit mystified, as if this kind of subject was foreign to her. Nevertheless, I got the impression that she was responsive to what I was saying.

Since that time, I am convinced in my spirit that Martina has followed through and become a Christian. It's an uncanny impression that I have not been able to dismiss. What her circumstances are, and where she is, I am ignorant of. However, I expect to meet Martina in the Lord's presence some day. And I will ask her, "Martina, how did God work in your life to bring you to faith in Christ? And what was your experience of living out that faith as a Christian?"

NORM AND FAY – (I'll include them as one person.)

They sat at our table for dinner on the cruise ship. Norm and Fay, Australians on their way to Alaska, as were my wife Marge and I. We had embarked in July 2015 on the Grand Princess cruise ship. They were a pleasant couple, quite conversational. We chatted about many things – life in our respective homes, family, work before retirement. For being Aussies, their English was easily understandable. Out of the blue, Norm ventured that he "was not very religious." I asked him he meant by that.

It sparked a lengthy conversation touching on creation, morality, authenticity of the Bible, and God, if there was a God. Faye said she didn't believe there was any beginning or end. And she was convinced that she had done nothing wrong. Contradicting herself, she offered her view that God will just love her, and when she gets "there" she will correct him as to what he has done wrong! When Faye said she didn't think she had wronged anyone, including God, I explained that sin, as depicted in the Eden scene, was really rebellion against God. Adam and Eve were telling God, "We don't want you to tell us what to do." All moral failure is really a symptom of sin. I further explained that the essence of sin was a person saying "I don't want God in my life." I saw a stunned look on her face, for both she and Norm had made it quite clear that they did not want God to interfere in their lives. It seemed to register with her that she indeed had done wrong to God. Norm claimed agnosticism, saying the Bible was basically fable.

We were not getting anywhere and I didn't want to be argumentative. So I ended by challenging Norm and Fay, as I did Martina, "When you think about God, say 'I want to know you better, and keep saying it.'" We parted for the evening. We never encountered Norm and Fay again.

I'm convinced God placed them at our table. It was no coincidence. I have confidence that, in whatever myriad of ways God can work, he is bringing them to faith in Christ. When I see them in heaven, I want to ask them how the process of believing came about. I will also want to know what their reaction was to that evening we spent at dinner on the Grand Princess.

THOR –

In Norse mythology the god Thor, son of Odin, was the god of thunder and lightning. He was associated with strength and storms. Fierce-eyed with red hair and beard, he was quick to anger, renowned for using his hammer to subdue enemies. In April 2008 I encountered a Thor seated beside me on a plane from Amsterdam to Minneapolis. That was his name. He was not a formidable, fierce-eyed man but a young Norwegian, 28 years old. We conversed a bit, and he offered that he was engaged in television work in Los Angeles. After that we both turned to separate pursuits. I began to read, actually in my Greek New Testament. Thor, curious about what I was reading, asked what language it was. I told him, "Greek." I added that I found truth and deep satisfaction for my life in God and his Word. Thor said at that, "I'm not into religion." I tried to explain more, that it was not about religion but a personal relationship with a loving God. His response was, "It all comes out as religion."

I dropped the subject, again not wanting to argue. Before landing, as we were retrieving our carry-ons, I said to him, "Thor, I'm sorry you had to sit beside a weird Christian. But someday you are going to need God." "Oh, I doubt it," he replied, "It's all a figment of the imagination." I left him with this challenge: "When you think about God, tell him you want to know him better." Again, Thor rejected the suggestion, saying, "I don't think that will happen." We parted and went separate ways.

Again, it was not a coincidence that Thor sat next to me on that flight. My confidence has grown that God has been and will continue to be at work in Thor's life. Thor challenged God by saying he didn't need him. I believe God will accept that challenge, and prove to him that indeed he does need God. How that will happen I don't know, but God understands just what it will take to bring Thor to humbly acknowledge Jesus as Lord. When I see him in heaven, I will ask him: how did God convince you of your need for him? And what has been your experience in life to live out that relationship with him?

Five people I want to see. And, of course, there are many other people I want to see in heaven as well.

"Who has measured the waters
in the hollow of His hand
and marked off the heavens with a span,
enclosed the dust of the earth
in a measure and weighed the mountains
in scales and the hills in a balance?"
Isaiah 40:12

19.

FLOCK OF GOATS

Song of Solomon 4:1

"Your hair is like a flock of goats
leaping down the slopes of Gilead."

1. The hair of her head
   Is the crown of her being.
   But what was Solomon
   Actually seeing?

2. A flock of goats,
   Jostling and leaping,
   Down a steep slope,
   Baaing and bleating?

3. Riches on hoof,
   Sees the man who owns goats;
   Fine wool for his robes,
   And beautiful coats.

4. That flock coursing down,
   Was so highly prized,
   A sure source of boasting
   To anyone's eyes.

5. Those flowing dark locks
   Enraptured the king.
   Their beauty and richness
   Made his heart sing.

6. He saw sinuous strands,
   Rippling over her head,
   Like a flock of rich wool,
   Streaming down Gilead.

20.

FOREST MAJESTIC

(At Forestville State Park, Minnesota)

It sounds so ordinary – a forest walk. But a forest has a majesty all its own. A glory permeates its being. That's not accidental, for with those who have eyes to see, "*The whole earth is full of His glory.*" The majesty and glory of this forest are in a sense forbidding. I am unwelcome there, intruding on sacred space. Without a reverent attitude, I am in a sense desecrating a holy place.

The depth and intricacy of a forest is impossible to fully grasp. I cannot begin to know what all these interlocking plants are, how they grow, how they differ from one another, what they contribute to the total aura. They grow. They interact. They live individually but form a cohesion. All of which does not include me. I am an outsider. They exist happily, expressing themselves in leaf and trunk and flower. They would live out their lives whether I or anyone else observed or cared.

There is an unseen energy that moves these organisms from birth to death. Not dramatic bursts of energy but slow and steady. One could watch for hours and see no notable change. Changes would manifest themselves unmistakably, though, over months and years. Forests are slow-motion entities. It was not by accident that J. R. R. Tolkien, when he introduced into the Lord of the Rings saga those strange tree-creatures he called Ents, made them slow, ponderous, lumbering beings. They had a deliberate rhythm to them, unlike that of "hasty" humans, elves or even hobbits. The forest is not in a hurry, and those who are in a hurry can never really appreciate it.

Though the forest is alive, there is death in the forest as well. Does God love the color green best? He has given us so much of it. That color signifies life, something that is alive. Planted in the midst of a forest, green abounds in every direction and on every level. Look high – leaves spring from the far extended boughs of a tree, arms reaching, reaching, reaching. Look low – small plants and shrubs of every shape and greenish hue blanket the forest floor. Large leaves spread out as massive hands. Small leaves array themselves in symmetry along a slender straw. They crisscross one another, forming an almost impenetrable wall, as if to reinforce that whisper, "Humans, you are not welcome to enter our world."

In the midst of all the greenness, decay presents its face. Plants die. A withered leaf, a fallen branch rotting into extinction. A tree, toppled from its roots, slowly, slowly succumbing to death's forces, returning to the ground from whence it came. But in the decay and degeneration there is hope. For it is a cycle, instilled in forest life by its Creator. The plant dies. It gradually decays. And at the end of the process, it becomes soil again on the forest floor. Fertile soil, life-giving soil. There is ample energy in that new soil to enable seeds to germinate and grow into mature trees and plants.

In the living and dying of a forest, our God prefigured the same cycle for those "made-in-His-image" creatures, who are dying, who need a renewal in the face of their death. He has promised to *"make all things new"*, and that promise comes even to humans who embrace the new life offered through Jesus Christ. The great apostle Paul wrote, *"If anyone is in Christ, that person is a new creation"* (2 Corinthians 5:17).

There is a mustiness in the forest air. Degeneration pulls the living vege-
tation down, down, down as it dies. It is a pleasant mustiness that compels
one to stop and breathe deeply. The appeal to eyesight in the forest is arrest-
ing in itself, with all its beauty to behold. But with eyes closed, the aromas
of the forest have an attraction all their own. One has to stop, just stop and
savor the air, filling the lungs over and over, before fully appreciating such
unfamiliar scents.

As if the majesty before one's eyes, and the aroma of forest life were not
enough, what catches the ears only compounds the pleasure. At first one
thinks there is only silence. Here in this cathedral of glory, at last there is
blessed silence. But then one realizes that our common life outside the forest
is permeated with a cacophony of sound, bombarding us at every turn. The
forest is so quiet. Listen to the quietness. Walking the earthen path is sound-
less. An unnatural quiet. But then, but then, as one stops and just listens,
sounds manifest themselves, some almost unobtrusively. What is that low
burbling? Ah, the stream, just through the trees, swift and bubbling along.
And listen, the leaves are singing. When a waft of wind arises, they offer a
chorus of rustling and murmuring. And it's antiphonal! First over here, then
over there. Arising in volume, falling away only to swell again. And that's not
all that graces one's hearing. The birds! Now, now one hears them. They form
a background chorus to the leafy song. A chirping here, a rill of song there,
a cawing, a melodious mating call. Most of the birds stay hidden, unseen

among the trees. Their sound blends well into the quiet undramatic flow of life in the forest. It is harmonious.

All forests belong to him, our Creator who knows how to make a forest display his glory. He who knows how to instill in forest life its cycle of life and death. He who created it all so that he could savor its majesty in sight and smell and sound for himself. He who in kindness allows us to share in what he Himself finds so joyfully pleasing.

We are privileged to stand in awe with such majesty surrounding us!

21.

ON THE THANKFULNESS OF GOD

Is God ever thankful? Is there such a thing as thankfulness in God?

From an early age, most parents teach their children to be thankful. The Scriptures exhort us to thankfulness repeatedly. In Old Testament writings, giving thanks to God constituted an integral element in worship, especially in Psalms, where the psalmists thank God for his steadfast love, for his majesty, for his goodness.

In the New Testament, the apostle Paul seemed to think gratitude to others was a singularly important virtue. It defined a Christian more clearly than anything else except love. His letter to the Colossians alone finds him encouraging thankfulness: to God the Father (1:12); [be] overflowing with thanks (2:7); be thankful (3:15); sing with heart-filled gratitude (3:16); give thanks to God (3:17); be thankful (4:2). In 1 Thessalonians 5:17, Paul challenged believers to give thanks even in all circumstances!

Even Jesus had the spirit of thankfulness. At both mass feeding miracles he lifted his face toward heaven and gave thanks for the loaves and fishes. In an upper room, at that Last Supper, he presented the bread as his body and the wine as his shed blood. For each he offered thanks.

If thankfulness is a major Christian virtue, ordered in the pages of God's Word, can we ascribe the same virtue to God? Is it appropriate to attribute gratitude to God? And if God is indeed a person of gratitude, why is there no mention of it in Scripture? Is thankfulness only offered from the lesser person to the greater? Would a king thank his subjects? Should a master thank his servants?

My thoughts on a thankful God were triggered by a selection from a devotional book "His Thoughts Said...His Father Said" by Amy Carmichael. She writes of an imagined conversation between a believer, a "son", and his Heavenly Father. In one piece, Carmichael cited a verse about Jesus being *"anointed with the oil of gladness"* (Psalm 45:7 Hebrews 1:9). She writes, "And then – and this was a word of wonder to the son – he heard his Father say clearly, 'I thank you for your joy.'" Amy Carmichael saw God as being thankful. Did she have insight into God's heart that we have missed? Would the Father really say to us "I thank you for..."?

Another clue comes from a parable Jesus told in Luke 12:35-37: *"Stay dressed for action and keep your lamps burning, and be like men who are waiting for their master to come home from the wedding feast, so that they may open the door to him at once when he comes and knocks. Blessed are those servants whom the master finds awake when he comes. Truly, I say to you, he will dress himself for service and have them recline at table, and he will come and serve them."*

The picture is of a householder, "the master", who came home very late from a wedding party. He was stunned to find his servants waiting up for him, ready to attend to his needs. Amazingly, the master invited the servants to sit down at the dining table, and he himself would serve <u>them</u> a meal! The story drips with the sense of thankfulness the householder has toward his servants for their willingness to meet his needs, even late at night. Clearly, the parable presents God as a thankful master.

The Scriptures state we are made in the image of God, and are quite insistent that we practice the grace of gratitude, regardless of circumstances. If then we are in the image of God, shouldn't we find an aspect of gratitude in God himself?

A spirit of gratitude arises out of a humble heart and a respect toward others. Thankfulness and humility travel together. Thankfulness arises when a person has received an object or act of service from another. I receive a gift for my birthday; I thank the one who gave it. Someone offers me a ride;

I thank them for offering. In each case, I exercise humility in being thankful. No one is compelled to give me anything or to serve me. When I offer thanks, I humble myself. A king, receiving an act of service from a commoner, shows humility in extending thanks.

So, is God humble? It appears that he is. In the person of his Son, he took human form and presented himself as a lowly servant of mankind. Jesus said of himself, *"I am meek and lowly* [humble] *of heart"* (Matthew 11:29). Jesus, the Son of God, the Author of Life, as Peter called him, chose to surrender his life in shame on a cross, a humbling choice and a humiliating sight. And the fact that God is constantly portrayed as one who "stoops" to care for his children shows a humility in him. David frequently wrote of God as our help, as in Psalm 63:7: *"You have been my help..."* His helpfulness accentuates his humility.

If God possesses aspects of thankfulness, why are there no explicit references to it in Scripture? Perhaps because the orientation of the Bible, in the face of an idolatrous world, emphasizes the exaltation of God as the Supreme Only God. The cultures of the time presented their deities as not much more than super humans, having all the flaws and idiosyncrasies that humans do. The God presented in the Bible is One *"high and lifted up"*; he is Almighty, Sovereign; he is holy beyond words. If the Scriptures portrayed him as thankful, some people might get the impression he was weak and fawning, simply trying to incur the favor of humans. Humble gods wouldn't get much press in the ancient world. But our Scriptures insist on both images of God – the Lofty One, and the gracious One, a Shepherd who tenderly stoops to help his lambs. Jesus identified himself as of a lowly, that is, humble nature (Matthew 11:29).

How does God express gratitude? Maybe in what we refer to as "God's blessings". God blesses his children. The blessings, including his grace and forgiveness, stimulate a thankful spirit in us. In return for that gratitude, God pours out more blessings. More blessings, more thankfulness. Thus, gratitude flows in both directions. Paul writes to the Corinthian church about the dynamics of blessings (grace) and gratitude: *"For it is all for your sake, so that as grace extends to more and more people it may increase thanks-*

giving, to the glory of God" (2 Corinthians 4:15). Grace and gratitude. Gratitude and grace. They work in a reciprocal pattern. A pattern that God himself enters into.

Does it make a difference? If I know that God is thankful, might my diligence in service to him be more intense, knowing he would be thankful for it? Surely the servants mentioned in Luke 12 would be more eager to wait on their master the next time he came home late, because he was thankful, treating them with grateful honor. Is God grateful that I pursue being like his Son? We can believe so. Being aware of that might motivate me to greater effort. If God is thankfully pleased by my intentions and efforts, the desires of my heart are therefore strengthened.

OUR GOD IS A THANKFUL GOD!!

22.

GOD'S HANDS — MY HANDS — Psalm 143:1-8

The Psalmist David wrote, *"I meditate on all your works, and consider what your hands have done. I spread out my hands to you..."* (vs. 5-6). He spoke of God's hands as active. It's a human comparison, of course. God has been "working", doing things in the world. He is a God who is busy, not an idle deity, passively waiting for his created beings to attend to him.

There are plenty of works of God to be contemplated. Some people see them; many do not. The most obvious works are right in front of us, the wonders of the created world: trees, grass, flowers, mountains, clouds, stars, the movements of the atmosphere, oceans, sun and moon. He has filled our world with evidence of his working hands. From all these commonplace aspects of nature to the more spectacular vistas and colorful extravagances of the sky. The less obvious works of God have to do with his providential sustaining of our lives: breath, strength of body, health, food, shelter, friends, jobs, family. All these are intended to focus our thoughts on a working God.

Implicit in David's words, and amply supported by other Scriptures, is the great truth that God's working is on behalf of his people. And he always acts with goodness toward us. In verse 8, David explicitly asked that he may know God's deep love right away in the morning. He expects God to act that way daily. God is not selfishly fixed on himself in his works. They are meant to highlight him as a God who cares for his people. When we praise him, we are achieving the highest level of blessing for ourselves. God's works are done for our joy and praise.

In contrast to the reference of God's active hands, David himself can only *"spread out his hands"* to God. He had nothing to claim by way of great works. No gifts to offer to God like that which God gives to us. David's hands were simply extended, open, the hands of a beggar asking for what God has to give. It was a gesture of humility. "Nothing in my hands I bring..." was a posture David was well acquainted with. He was a "poor-in-spirit" man. Jesus said such people were happy, blessed. The principle of Jesus holds true: *"Everyone who exalts himself will be humbled, and everyone who humbles himself will be exalted."* Here we have a man of spiritual poverty, without great works, humbly extending his hands to the God who himself works with his own hands.

When David presented this image of extending his hands as a beggar, he reinforced it with: *"My soul thirsts for you as in a parched land"* (vs. 6). It is not coincidental that David connected his own thirsty soul with meditating on the God who works. Observation of and pondering the handiwork of God pulls me toward him. It's a pull that wants even more experience of God. Thus, David craved further awareness of the God who works for his people. Not only did David's soul thirst, but he emphasized the effect by adding, "*my spirit faints within me*" (vs. 7). To David, if he did not "get" more of God, his very spirit would suffer.

In an urgent response to God, maybe fearful that God will not take note of his "soul thirst", David boldly appealed, "*Do not hide your face from me...*" (vs. 7b). As was noted, he stressed his need for greater reassurance of God who works on his behalf: "*Let the morning bring me word of your unfailing love, for I have put my trust in you*" (vs. 8). David's appeal to God was, "If you are a God who works, then may your work reveal every morning that you love me with an unconditional love, an insistent, never-ending love."

What an amazing approach David had to God. He fixed his mind on an active, energetic God who loved him, knowing that he, David, had nothing to offer God comparable with such grace. He only knew his soul wanted more and more of his God.

23.

GOD OF THE LAND -
Psalm 65:9-13

"You care for the land and water it; you enrich it abundantly. The streams of God are filled with water to provide the people with grain, for so you have ordained it. You drench its furrows and level its ridges; you soften it with showers and bless its crops. You crown the year with your bounty, and your carts overflow with abundance. The grasslands of the wilderness overflow; the hills are clothed with gladness. The meadows are covered with flocks and the valleys are mantled with grain; they shout for joy and sing."

Do we know what God thinks of his earth? What does he care about? We find the Psalmist David writing of God, *"You care for the land..."* (NIV). The ESV and KJV use the term *"visit"* instead of *"care for"*, but the Hebrew word bears the idea of attending to something with favorable intent, even to carefully managing it. Thus, the NIV phrase *"care for"* seems to capture what David meant to convey. It's a profound understanding of how God relates to his earth in a tangible and observable way. It presents a God who has an intense interest in his natural world but in a particular manner: he cares for the specific piece of land that people manage productively.

David could look out over the fields his people had cultivated. He saw the furrows and ridges left by the plow. He observed how rains softened the ridges. In his mind, he saw how God energized the soil, and the scattered seed, to produce welcome grain. David saw uncultivated land as well – grasslands and meadows dotted with flocks of sheep and goats, vineyards bursting with grapes. These too come under the care of God. God has an interest in the ordinary acts of planting and reaping and herding. When David thought of God's care for his land, he noted how God is interested in its productivity: "*You crown the year with your bounty, and your carts overflow with abundance*." The God who cares for his land is delighted by what his people can produce through it. David saw God's delight in the hills that are "*clothed with gladness*". The valleys that set off the glad hills also "*shout and sing for joy.*"

Interestingly, David gave us a picture of a God who delights in a natural world not just for its own sake. He cares for the land when mankind is intricately involved with it. Some naturalist-oriented people hold the view that Nature is spoiled by man's presence. They view as ideal the preservation of land as wilderness, isolated stretches of land where no living person can set foot and thus despoil. They would be happy, it seems, if no human being would ever enjoy the land. One poem I studied in high school, "The Unnamed Lake", concerned an obscure lake visited by the poet Frederic George Scott. In his first verse, he noted how the lake seemed to be so isolated, as if no one had ever seen it. After observing the lake and some wildlife around it, the author concluded by quietly departing the way he came, without feeling the impulse to bestow a name on the lake, hence the title of his poem. He implied by the last line of his poem that applying a man-made name would somehow corrupt the pristine, pure character of this part of nature.

Reams of paper and hundreds of books have detailed how man has indeed destroyed and exploited and harmed the natural world. Tragically so! But Psalm 65 seems to say God's delight is in his land where humans are involved. Involved responsibly, as they plant and reap, as they graze flocks. These are but metaphors for thousands of activities where humanity uses the natural world to be beneficially productive. God is impressed when people take what he has given and make it fruitful in such a way that people benefit each other. In such a way, it can be seen that the natural world *"shouts for joy"*. The joy comes in how mankind produces so much that helps people live well.

Mankind may work gardens or lawns or tilled fields of corn or wheat, herd cattle on vast ranchlands, mine for metals, fish the seas, and a myriad of other activities. In that piece of earth that God has given to each, we can be assured that such actions delight God. Our lands *"shout for joy and sing."*

24.

MY HELP

In Psalm 70:5, David said to God, *"You are my help and my deliverer."* The word for "help" is *"ezer"*, the same Hebrew word used for Eve in Genesis 2:18, where God promised to make an *"ezer"* fit for Adam. Adam needed a helper. David's words imply that God stoops in humility to be our partner-helper. Two chapters before this, in 68:19, David described God as one who *"daily bears us up"*, the implication being he carries our burdens.

This picture of God as a helper is pervasive, especially in Psalms, where reference to God's help appears 48 times. This huge number communicates a truth that may elude me – the mighty God of all, the Creator of the universe, stands to help me. It's the picture of a humble God, who essentially puts himself at my service, a concept that many would protest. The opposite is supposed to be true – I am here to serve him. But he *"knows our frame; he remembers that we are dust"* (Psalm 103:14). So he helps me. It must have been a profound revelation to David and others that God was their helper. Especially in the face of the pagan religions surrounding them, whose gods didn't help. Instead, those gods demanded performance of sacrificial rituals before they would even offer any help at all. The worshipers of other gods had no confidence the gods would help them. David boldly declared that God's help is given freely, a gift of steadfast love. God the Lord is one who bears burdens, bears up his children. He is not too proud to be called a helper.

But considering God as a helper requires humility on the part of his children: the willingness to let God help. How often has my drive to be self-sufficient and independent closed me off from the joy of letting God help me? Many people resist having anyone help them. They will politely refuse any offers of assistance. They can get along quite nicely by themselves, thank you!

I was hunting with my son Ellick near Custer South Dakota. We tracked in different directions and agreed to meet at a certain point. He didn't show up at the appointed time. I was anxious, waiting, waiting. It was a big forest, and anyone could get lost easily. So I prayed, "Lord, what shall I do?" Immediately the line of a song swept through my mind: "I've no cause for worry or for fear". Then I was prompted to go to where he last was located. I noticed there his tracks in the snow, leading opposite from where they should have gone. Following the tracks in snow and mud, down a forest road to a main road, the line of the song kept me calmed. A group of hunters came by and I asked them to drive me to my vehicle. There beside my van was my son. Some other hunters had found him and driven him to our vehicle. God helped me.

God's people will praise him when they experience his help. David knew the process intimately: "*For you have been my help, and in the shadow of your wings I sing for joy*" (Psalm 63:7). Not accidently did he reference praise of God in 68:19: "*Praise be to the Lord...who daily bears us up*". I can't help but believe that our God is overjoyed himself in being allowed to help me when I call on him. And David found it a daily experience. The Message Bible phrases it as: "*day after day*".

If my concept of God's help is that its application is only for major problems and issues, the use of the word "daily" changes the picture. My day-to-day life does not generally issue in major challenges. Rather, most experience is mundane, routine and involving so-called minor hurdles and complaints. So I can conclude that God wants to help me in the insignificant daily things of life as well as a more traumatic event. Daily he is my "ezer"! And there is nothing about my daily life that cannot be included in his helping grace. The truth is not, "God helps those who help themselves." The truth is simply, for God's children, "God helps!"

"...the mountains and the hills before you shall break forth into singing, and all the trees of the field shall clap their hands."
Isaiah 55:12

25.

INAUDIBLE PRAISE
– Psalm 65:1

Can praise be silent?

The phrase "inaudible praise" is almost an oxymoron to a contemporary Christian generation. They may not even understand how that can be possible. Praise, as some are convinced, **has** to be audible. It has to be heard!

On that subject, David presents us with an interesting contrast in Psalm 65:1: *"Praise is due to you, O God, in Zion..."* The ESV footnotes this verse as *"Praise awaits you in silence, O God..."* The KJV simply says, *"Praise waiteth for thee, O God..."* The Hebrew word for "wait" means to wait silently. Eugene Peterson in The Message writes the verse as *"Silence is praise to you, Zion-dwelling God".* Can David mean that praise is possible when I am silent before God? If I just focus on him and his presence, is it really genuinely praising God? When I wait in silence before God, it is a way of acknowledging his sovereign status over all things, including me. As such it is indeed a form of praise.

What is interesting here is the idea that praise can be silent, without words, music, noise or clapping. Praise does not require audible expression. As mentioned, perhaps The Message version best captures the essence of David's words: *"Silence is praise..."*. We are not used to praise being silent.

Our "praise team" approach to a Sunday morning worship service accepts unquestionably the idea that praise requires an audible presentation. With some churches, that comes across as "the louder the better". Crashing cymbals with pounding drums. Booming bass guitars amped to uncomfortable decibels. A church I caught on live-streaming one Sunday had the pastor and music team shouting to each other, over and over and over, "Shout now! Shout now! Shout now!" Can a church that makes earplugs available during worship even conceive of the idea praise can be expressed in silence? Or a contemporary Christian music concert where it is assumed that praise must have decibel levels approaching a painful threshold? The inference seems to be that unless the noise level can almost deafen, praise is weak and inadequate. How uncomfortable it would be in a typical worship service if we were led in a moment, maybe minutes, of silent praise! Most of us wouldn't know how to handle such extended periods of silence.

Part of the difficulty in considering silent praise is that Scripture itself registers frequent occasions of praise being vocal. Before the throne of God, "four living creatures" engage in unceasing praise of God. They are joined by twenty-four elders, and then millions upon millions of angels singing and praising God and his Son (Rev 4-5). Apart from Psalm 65:1, David and other psalmists call us to praise God both verbally and instrumentally: "...I will praise you with the lyre, O God..." (43:4); "...his praise shall continually be in my mouth" (34:1); "Praise him with tambourine...with strings and pipe! Praise him with...loud-clashing cymbals!" (150:4-5).

However, can I not praise God while walking in quiet woods, fixed on God's presence, plodding quietly over rain-sodden leaves, conscious of no sounds except the tweet of a bird? Or contemplating a starry night sky, or a bold moon in its fullness? Or thrilling over the wonder of a little baby? The wonder of a colorful butterfly flitting from blossom to blossom can cause one to soundlessly offer praise to its Maker. When a landscape takes away my breath, or the murmur of an ocean shore mesmerizes the imagination, how fitting to sit in silent praise to God. Can quiet joy in the presence of a dear friend not be an offering of praise to God? There are myriads of other quiet experiences where the awareness of the beauty God has placed in front of us captivates our soul. Or times of reflection on how God has acted in providential love. Words, audible words, fail us. At such times, our spirit ascends to God with silent praise.

David appears to recognize the place of such silent praise when he addresses God in vs. 8: "*Those who dwell at the ends of the earth* [i.e., all peoples] *are in awe at your wonders*." Awe-prompted silence is powerful praise. David goes on to say to God: "*You make the going out of the morning and the evening to shout for joy*." That is, God's prompting of the sun's rising and its setting brings out joyful song. To us, the sunrise and the sunset make no audible sound. Scripture says praise is happening.

No tension need be felt between audible and inaudible praise. It's not one or the other. The expression of both fills out worship of God. But let us not be unaware that much praising can be done in a silent face-to-face meeting with God. He knows our hearts when words fail us.

26.
JESUS SOBBED - Luke 19:41:

"And when he drew near and saw
the city, he wept over it."

Jesus approached Jerusalem one last time. The end was in sight. He had just told his disciples, again, that he would be arrested, tortured, killed and then rise again. He was about to make a very public entry into Jerusalem, a parade down the slopes of the Mount of Olives. Jesus set up his entry as a way to bring the prophecy of Zechariah 9:9 into reality. The prophecy exhorts Jerusalem to rejoice at the coming of her Messiah King, a righteous man bringing salvation. He was to ride in on a colt, *"the foal of a donkey"*.

As he approached Jerusalem, Jesus sent two unnamed disciples to the next village where they would find a colt tied in a certain location. They were to untie the colt and bring it to Jesus.

When they brought the colt to Jesus, they put their cloaks on it and *"set Jesus on it"*, a colt that had never been ridden. The Old Testament Scriptures said this was one of the major signs of Messiah's coming to Jerusalem. Maybe all the disciples guessed by this time what was happening. Did they know the prophecy: *"Rejoice greatly, O daughter of Zion!...Behold, your king is coming to you...mounted on a colt?"* Maybe or maybe not.

However, the crowd knew something momentous was happening. They were in a celebratory mood, rejoicing, laying their cloaks down for Jesus' promenade down the slope of the Mount of Olives. Luke says it was *"the whole crowd of disciples"*. They loudly praised God with an Old Testament passage believed to be messianic, *"Blessed is he who comes in the Name of the Lord"* (Psalm 118:26).

It was a festive occasion. People rejoiced. Messiah-King, son of David (Mark 11:10) had broken into their time. What a breathtaking event! At last the new age had dawned, the fulfillment of all those Isaiah prophecies. What was next? How would this Messiah proceed? Would he march to the Antonia, the Roman garrison on the temple corner square, and oust them with the power of just a word? Would he go to Herod's palace and tell *"that fox"* (Luke 13:32) to pack up and leave? Oh, the excitement of it all! They praised their God. He had come through!

In the midst of such heightened celebration, with emotions running wild, Jesus approached the city itself. He paused as he saw the city walls and there beyond them, the temple in all its glory. But he was not rejoicing. What did the disciples observe now as they looked at him? He wept! The Messiah sobbed! The Greek word *"klaio"* refers to great heaving sobs, even wailing. We read in John 11:35 that Jesus also wept. But in contrast, his weeping there over Lazarus was more of a softer grieving, with silent tears.

Why did Jesus weep? Especially at this moment of messianic recognition? Messiahs were not supposed to weep. They were strong, mighty. The reality was that Jesus saw this event so much differently. The political messianic rule would not be ushered in right now, but instead a terrible devastation would ensue. Israel would herself suffer incredible defeat at the hands of the Romans rather than the Romans themselves being destroyed by Messiah. Jesus sobbed because this people in front of him had not recognized God's coming to them (vs. 44) in the person of Jesus. Paradoxically, the Kingdom would come, not in political power, but in the pending death and resurrection of Messiah King.

What brought Jesus to be wracked with sobs? Deep, full-hearted caring, mixed perhaps with frustration and disappointment. The clue is in vs. 42: *"If you had only known…"*. For three years, he had poured out his heart in teaching, preaching, healing for this people but they were still ignorant of how the way of Messiah's rule of peace would come for them. The religious authorities and most of the people rejected his kind of messiahship. Jesus foresaw that the end result would be devastation and suffering. Passion gripped him as he realized how tragically Israel had missed the whole point.

Passionate sobbing does not arise instantaneously. It is rather the culmination of long periods of yearning over one's circumstances or those which other persons are experiencing. Days and nights of caring, maybe hours of praying, begging God for a desired outcome.

Once again, the important factor is what one wants, and how much it is wanted. The degree of desire may only be a trivial: "Yeah, that would be nice to have." But the other extreme is an experience of craving, a yearning so intense that it essentially says, "I can't live without having that." It is the latter that generates heart-wrenching sobs of longing when the craving is frustrated. Was Jesus saying essentially, "I can't live without the saving of God's people?" If a person can live without acquiring some object of desire, they may soon lose interest in pursuing it. But if they cannot live without it, they will put their heart and energy into bringing it about. Jesus, according to Luke 9:51, *"set his face resolutely"* to go to Jerusalem. He had just told his disciples about his upcoming death. When Peter protested that this must never happen, Jesus vehemently challenged him, saying that Peter's alternative plan was inspired of Satan. Such vehemence reveals a passion for a desired outcome. He knew that what he had to give for these people, for their saving, was being rejected. Such passion erupted in a sobbing Jesus.

"He made the moon to mark the seasons"
(Psalm 104:19)

27.
LITTLE BOY WALK AT ¼ MPH

(my grandson Sebastian)

We kick at the leaves.
We pick up a stick.
We stomp on a grating,
We squat to check a tiny ant,
and say, "Aaeey".
We twirl round a tree, and a
                    lamppost.
            We pick a new stick.
          We wave at a truck and say,
                    "Eeeeh".
      We give our stick to a lady at the bus stop.
              We sit on the curb.
          We wave at a girl across the street.

We find a new stick.
We kick at a dirt pile.
We stomp splash in some water,
and squeal.
We climb on some large piping and pat it.
We peek through a hedge.
We pat the hedge, we pat the tree, we pat the
sidewalk.
We kick the green paper.
We pat a pickup's big tire.
We meet a lady in her yard.
We wave at the bus.
We climb a low fence.
We poke a finger in a hole in the lawn,
and say, "Eeeaay."
We toddle on home.
All in all, a good walk,
And a great gift from God!

28.

How Love Works -
Romans 8:35

"Who shall separate us from the love of Christ?"

When Paul asks in Romans 8:35, "*Who shall separate us from the love of Christ?*", he is referring to a common trait of love in the human realm – the fickleness of attraction between persons. When a love relationship exists, it has a certain fragility or maybe a temporality to it. Love is subject to change from outside forces. What originally attracted one person to another may no longer be operative at a later time. Some person might present a more attractive "face" and thus attention swings to that person. The one with the more attractive features and nature gains the attention of the other.

There is an inherent insecurity in being loved, on a human level, if it is perceived that love is based on my own appeal or charm. How can I guarantee that I will be as appealing tomorrow as I am today? Will the one who loves me fall subject to someone else's more magnetic appeal? What if the one who loves me finds less to love in me tomorrow and thus allows their love to diminish? What if someone with more allure and attractive qualities draws away the love first directed toward me?

These questions set up the possibility where I now have to compete for love. I have to curry favor with someone in order to ensure they will love me. I have to prove I am more appealing, more attractive, more worth loving than a perceived rival. So the pressure to perform arises, and I am tempted to love another person only in order to manipulate them into maintaining their love for me. But I can never be certain the effort to solicit love toward me will be sufficient. And how will I ever know? Thus, a vicious cycle arises, loving only for the purpose of being loved in return.

But Paul is saying that the love relationship with Jesus is totally different. The love Jesus expresses is entirely self-generated on his part. It is inherent within him, not dependent on any external impetus such as an attractiveness or appeal within me. The expected answer to Paul's question – *"Who shall separate us...?"* – is No One! Jesus does not love me because of something about me – goodness, personality, intelligence, diligence, effort, sacrifice and more. These are not elements that trigger his love toward me. He loves me because he has chosen to do so apart from outside influences.

Therefore, since no external circumstances stimulate Christ's love for me, neither can they alter that love. Love was not expressed because I attracted it, nor will it be withdrawn because I am in some way no longer appealing to him. Thus, his love is certain and stable, not fickle. No "rival" will draw his love and attention away from me. If there was nothing within me in the first place that prompted his interest, then nothing else, no one else, in all creation can present a more powerful basis for him to redirect his love and interest away from me.

How clear Paul is on this: *"Who [or what] can separate me from the love of Christ?"* Why, NOTHING, of course! Christ's love is not based on or affected by a someone or something outside of himself. What joy of confidence and security I can take from this truth. No wonder Paul waxes so eloquent in praising the steadfast love of Christ, closing his thoughts with, *"For I am sure that nor height nor depth, nor anything else in all creation, will be able to separate us from the love of God in Christ Jesus our Lord."*

I AM SECURE IN THE LOVE OF CHRIST!

"Arise, shine, for your light has come,
and the glory of the Lord has risen upon you.
Isaiah 60:1"

29.
MAY DELIGHT

Any May day is God's gift to your soul!
You savor each one with delight!
How its magic enlivens your senses,
Filling your heart day and night.

A velvety green carpets the lawn,
And captures your eyes with its glory.
Birds flitting and chirping trumpet their song —
Nature's ever romantic story.

Eager shoots push dark soil aside.
They promise a new world aglow.
Are they hostas? Tulips? Or lilies?
You can't wait to boast of their show.

Go to the shed and get out that rake!
Attack those dead leaves on the ground!
Swinging, pulling, stir up musty smells,
Building mound after mound after mound.

And what's that deafening silence of sound?
The bugs? Can you find one anywhere?
No buzzing and whirring, no bites on the arms.
Let maximum skin be made bare!

No time for a nap; no time for TV!
Let no moment of May go to waste.
Call in sick! Take a park walk!
Fresh air in the lungs? Oh, embrace!

Warm breezes caress open face,
And tease strands of free-flowing tresses.
Oh, bask in rain's smell on the grass,
Just a sample of how our God blesses.

Winter and summer, autumn and spring!
Each season unique in its way.
The months reflecting God's faithful care,
But none is so special as May!

30.
MOMENTOUS ENCOUNTER
– Isaiah 6:1-8

"In the year that King Uzziah died I saw the Lord sitting upon a throne, high and lifted up; and the train of his robe filled the temple. Above him stood the seraphim. Each had six wings: with two he covered his face, and with two he covered his feet, and with two he flew. And one called to another and said: "Holy, holy, holy is the LORD of hosts; the whole earth is full of his glory!" And the foundations of the thresholds shook at the voice of him who called, and the house was filled with smoke. And I said: 'Woe is me! For I am lost; for I am a man of unclean lips, and I dwell in the midst of a people of unclean lips; for my eyes have seen the King, the LORD of hosts!' Then one of the seraphim flew to me, having in his hand a burning coal that he had taken with tongs from the altar. And he touched my mouth and said: 'Behold, this has touched your lips; your guilt is taken away, and your sin atoned for.' And I heard the voice of the Lord saying, "Whom shall I send, and who will go for us?" Then I said, 'Here I am! Send me.'"

Isaiah said to God, "Here I am!" It was after a momentous, unimaginable encounter with God. Isaiah was responding to a question he heard the Lord Almighty ask: *"Whom shall I send? Who will go for us?"* It was an indirect question, appearing not to be asked of Isaiah himself. But Isaiah answered the question anyway, believing that, in some way, it was indeed meant for him. He offered himself without knowing what he was offering himself for. Presenting himself for whatever was being asked of him was spontaneous. He stood before the Lord Almighty (lit. "Yahweh of heavenly armies") and dared to volunteer himself for what Yahweh the King wanted of him. Isaiah placed himself at the King's disposal.

Isaiah did not come to this point easily or voluntarily at first. His response came out of a dramatic, even traumatic, experience before the Lord asked the question. Isaiah was worshiping in the temple. He had been a faithful follower of Yahweh so his presence at the temple was not unusual. This was an ordinary event for him. Was he in the priestly caste? A Levite? We do know he was specifically identified as a prophet in the books of Kings and Chronicles. We could presume he had been in the temple many times, offering sacrifices of worship to his God. He was accustomed to the rituals: animals killed and butchered, their blood pouring out and sprinkled on the altar, and even on him. The smells of roasting flesh, of incense and blood permeated the air. It was all so familiar to Isaiah. He was a devout and righteous man. The worship of God and being righteous before him had always been of paramount importance.

He was committed to Yahweh, this God of ancient Israel. Isaiah knew the history, the ebb and flow of Israel's spiritual life. But all he knew of God was that story, and the theologies and writings. How Yahweh dealt with an Abraham, a Jacob, a Moses. He knew the exploits of the great king David some 300 years earlier and his poetic songs offered to God. He felt the awesomeness of the temple scene, including its critical place in Israel's life. In his visits to the temple, he could sense in some way that God inhabited that place, especially in the Holy of Holies.

But for Isaiah, and indeed for most Israelites, there was a remoteness to this God. Who was he? Why had he not shown himself in more dramatic ways? Maybe the Israelite people would have behaved more righteously if Yahweh had appeared to them visibly and frequently. Would they have been more faithful then? Isaiah may have in fact yearned for Israel to repent and follow Yahweh exclusively, spending his time in the temple praying for just that situation to come to pass. So where was this God? Perhaps Isaiah was pondering these thoughts as he knelt in prayer and worship.

His heart was heavy in one sense. The good king Uzziah had just died, having reigned for 52 years. His was a reign where *"he did what was right in the eyes of the LORD"*. He had *"set himself to seek the Lord."*

Suddenly, the natural realm broke open and a different reality hit Isaiah like a clap of thunder. *"I saw the Lord..."* Four words spoken simply, but projecting a scene like he had never ever encountered before. No one had seen the Lord! It was forbidden, and impossible. Yes, Moses had sort of seen the Lord, only Moses, but that was 500 years ago. What was going on? Isaiah's eyes were opened to a new reality, a reality hidden from him until then. He saw God! God on his throne, elevated above him, high and lifted up.

In the imagery of royalty, Isaiah saw God clothed with a majestic, full-flowing robe. In fact, so magnificent and massive was his robe that it was said to fill the temple. The message was: the presence of God overwhelms all boundaries. Amazingly, in this vision, as in the visions of the book of Revelation, the Lord God is never alone. He comes accompanied by other beings: *"Above him stood the seraphs..."* He is glorified, and his majesty enhanced, by these spiritual beings around him.

In Isaiah's view the seraphs had wings, each with six of them. *"...with two they were flying..."*, Isaiah wrote. Why would spiritual beings need wings? Perhaps wings were meant to convey symbolically that such a being operated outside the bounds of normal physical limitations. Oddly, the other two pair of wings provided a covering for face and feet. To add to the eerie scene, Isaiah noted the seraphs were calling to each other. Not to Isaiah. Not even to the Lord God. In a posture of worship, they called to each other. A melodious chanting of praise to God. There is a hint of timelessness to their act – a constant, on-going, never-ceasing preoccupation. John the Apostle in his vision also observed *"four living creatures"* before the throne of God, each having six wings as well. They too called without ceasing, voicing the same words as the seraphs Isaiah heard: *"Holy, holy, holy is the Lord God,"* adding *"Who was, and is, and is to come"* (Revelation 4:8). Isaiah heard an additional line: *"The whole earth is full of his glory."* Both accounts would have us see that the Lord God dwells in an atmosphere of never-ending praise and devotion from his creation. No doubt joy accompanied the seraphs' praise, as did the Lord's reception of that praise.

Such praise and worship have power. Isaiah watched in awe and terror as the seraphs' voices actually shook the temple structures of wood and stone. Doorposts and thresholds trembled. Massive stones and pillars could not stand firm when angels praised. And smoke, from somewhere, filled the room. It was an eerie, other-worldly, and frightening scene for Isaiah. Perhaps he was thinking, "I have to get out of here!" Yet he was transfixed by the incredible awesomeness of that scene, held spellbound in the presence of God.

Isaiah couldn't move. He felt crushed by the weight of the glory of the Lord God. In fact, he considered his life at an end: *Woe is me! I am undone!*" It was the equivalent of saying, "Oh no! It's all over for me!" Isaiah fully expected to die. Two impressions confronted him: the horror of his and Israel's sin, and the fact that he had seen the Lord Almighty. The holiness of God burned with an intensity that made his sin intolerable. The admission was spontaneous. He could not contain himself. Holiness would consume all that was unholiness. Isaiah suddenly felt the burden of the words, words, words spoken by him and the nation, words so in contradiction to the holy words of God. Those alone should seal his fate. He knew instinctively that our words reveal the state of one's heart. But additionally, just seeing God was a death sentence. "*No man can see God and live*," was the unanimous view of the Israelite people.

Then amazingly, Isaiah watched a seraph fly to him. It had a hot coal in his hand, taken with tongs from the altar where Isaiah had been offering up a sacrifice. The seraph carrying a live coal produced no smell of burning flesh to Isaiah. What would the seraph do? Why would he, a holy angel, approach him? Isaiah was an unclean man among all these unclean worshipers around him. A hot coal to the lips seemed abhorrent, but that's exactly what the seraph was doing: "*See, this has touched your lips...*". Again, Isaiah experienced no burning flesh. The seraph spoke further, "*...your guilt is taken away and your sin atoned for.*" And then he was gone. And Isaiah was left to wonder how a live fiery coal could take away his sin, or atone for it. Had the seraph asked the Majestic One on the throne for permission to grant forgiveness? How could Isaiah be certain that his sins were indeed forgiven?

At some level, Isaiah must have reasoned that the seraph used the coals of the altar in a more deeply personal way than what he was accustomed to. He often sacrificed, and the written promises of God through Moses assured the worshiper of cleansing and forgiveness. But somehow the ritual never quite touched his heart, assuring an absolute forgiveness. What the seraph did – physically touching his lips with a live coal –symbolized a deep cleansing, a burning away of the sin caused by the offending member of his body. That coal – one of many coals – had consumed the offering on the altar. Now the seraph's action effected a consuming of the sin that burdened Isaiah.

He felt cleansed as he had never experienced before. The proof is in his immediate response to the question, *"Who will go…?"* Just moments before, Isaiah stood paralyzed with guilt and shame, feeling his unworthiness to stand before the holy Lord Almighty. Now he can offer himself readily for whatever was being asked of him: *"Here I am!"* He did not hesitate. His sin was no longer a detriment to serving God. His subsequent ministry as a prophet of God – speaking for him with cleansed lips - would not be hindered by the crushing awareness of sins past. The atoning power of God, through the seraph's action, had liberated him.

31.

MY SOUL – MY GLORY

King David glories in the word "glory". His psalms express the Hebrew word *kabod* with uncommon frequency. Most occurrences apply to the Lord: *"Who is this King of glory? The Lord, strong and mighty..."* (Psalm 24:10); *"The heavens declare the glory of God..."* (19:1). It is easy to grasp how the word defines God. It's basic meaning of "weightiness" leads to the idea of "impressiveness". What is weighty can make a dent in something, an impression. The concept of splendor soon comes to mind as well. All such thoughts combine to highlight the greatness and majesty of God.

David writes: *"I have set the Lord always before me; because he is at my right hand I shall not be shaken"* (16:8). Then he makes a conclusion, using *kabod* in a curious way: *"Therefore my heart is glad, and my kabod rejoices; my body also dwells secure"* (vs 9). The ESV translates this as *"...my whole being rejoices...."* Other translators use the word "soul". The KJV accurately translates the verse: *"...my glory rejoices..."* Why the word "glory" where we might would expect the word "soul"?

Was this just a solitary quirk in language by the Psalmist? Did he misuse a word? Should he have realized he was being somewhat confusing? If it were only in Psalm 16:9 where we find this curious usage, we might indeed think David was being imprecise. However, upon exploring other Psalms, we find at least three other occasions where David writes in the same way, using *kabod* which other English versions translate as "soul", "whole being" , "heart":

"You have turned for me my mourning into dancing; you have loosed my sackcloth and clothed me with gladness, that my kabod *may sing your praise and not be silent"* (30:11-12).

"Awake, my kabod !" (57:8)

"My heart is steadfast, O God! I will sing and make melody with my kabod ["whole being" ESV]!" (108:1)

The question naturally arises: why does David use the word normally translated "glory" but English versions render it most commonly as "soul"? Does David regard the word "glory" as a synonym for one's soul? Maybe the basic meaning of *kabod* as weightiness or impressiveness helps us understand. God's glory is his impressiveness, his essential greatness. Honor and splendor radiate from him. His glory catches our attention and attracts us, even creating unspeakable awe. His essence, that is, his very soul, is gloriously impressive.

Might it be what David applied on a human level as well? When the word *kabod* is used for soul, it refers to the essential person within each of us. That inner person, the real "me", is impressive. It carries weight. With it we make an impact in the world around us.

My soul, the real me, is my glory. God made each of us unique, which in itself makes us impressive. No one else in all the history of creation is like me. I am one of a kind. The fact that God made only one person like me, and discarded the mold, is a huge honor he pays to me. The same can be said of each one of us. And when God honors me with a uniqueness that becomes impressive, it is my glory. How fitting then that my special uniqueness in turn reflects back on God, highlighting his glory in creating me! Can we not ask that God would take the uniqueness of our souls, our glory, and impress other people with the impressiveness of God?

32.
PROTECTION OR PRESENCE? – Psalm 27

"The LORD is my light and my salvation; whom shall I fear? The LORD is the stronghold of my life; of whom shall I be afraid?

When evildoers assail me to eat up my flesh, my adversaries and foes, it is they who stumble and fall.

Though an army encamp against me, my heart shall not fear; though war arise against me, yet I will be confident.

One thing have I asked of the LORD, that will I seek after: that I may dwell in the house of the LORD all the days of my life, to gaze upon the beauty of the LORD and to inquire in his temple.

For he will hide me in his shelter in the day of trouble; he will conceal me under the cover of his tent; he will lift me high upon a rock.

And now my head shall be lifted up above my enemies all around me, and I will offer in his tent sacrifices with shouts of joy; I will sing and make melody to the LORD.

Hear, O LORD, when I cry aloud; be gracious to me and answer me!

You have said, 'Seek my face.' My heart says to you, 'Your face, LORD, do I seek.'

Hide not your face from me. Turn not your servant away in anger, O you who have been my help. Cast me not off; forsake me not, O God of my salvation!

For my father and my mother have forsaken me, but the LORD will take me in.

Teach me your way, O LORD, and lead me on a level path because of my enemies.

Give me not up to the will of my adversaries; for false witnesses have risen against me, and they breathe out violence.

I believe that I shall look upon the goodness of the LORD in the land of the living!

Wait for the LORD; be strong, and let your heart take courage; wait for the LORD!"

In Psalm 27:4 David wrote that there is one thing he wanted to ask of the Lord. It's not a casual request, for the Hebrew word means to beg, even demand. That one thing was his heart's desire: *"to dwell in the house of the Lord"* as long as he lives. The house of the Lord at first glance is a reference to the tabernacle. But further reference identifies it as the place where God is present. So, David's request was to be intimately present with the Lord, to experience God's presence with him. He followed that by expressing an equally strong desire: *"to gaze on the beauty of the Lord"*.

David opened his Psalm by writing about his enemies advancing on him. They were besieging him, threatening his life. But David was confident that the Lord was his stronghold, his fortified refuge. He had protection. He was guarded against his enemies. But suddenly David switched his thought away from safety and security to what his heart most desired – a personal experience of the Lord himself. He wanted to know God's presence intimately. He wanted to feast his eyes on the Lord's beauty, the Hebrew word referring to delight and pleasantness. It seemed David had made a significant leap in spiritual maturity.

One basic human need is to feel secure, safe. We want to live without fear of harm. David began his Psalm expressing that desire. "Lord, protect me..." However, he transitioned his thinking from a desire for protection to a more spiritually basic heart-hunger: to know God's presence and to live with constant delight in his attractiveness. *"One thing have I asked of the LORD, that will I seek after: that I may dwell in the house of the LORD all the days of my life, to gaze upon the beauty of the LORD and to inquire in his temple.*

Much of Christian living focuses on getting help and security from the Lord. The emphasis is on the trials that beset us. We pray for help in the face of these "enemies" – the ills and woes of life. We want protection from these before they overcome us. At that level, we simply want basic human needs to be met, and believe that God is willing and able to intervene. Which he is. But it's another level entirely to move from wanting protection from the ills of life, relief from our trial-enemies, to wanting the Lord for who he is in himself. Just to know him and revel in his presence and beauty.

In verse, 8 David recognized that his heart compelled him to seek the face of God. And he most passionately wanted to follow through on this desire. But will God "*hide his face*" from him? In other words, David was aware that God had ample reason to withhold his presence, not allowing an intimate connection. However, he became convinced that if he drew near to God, he would not suffer rejection.

But now again, David's mind moved to his need for protection: "*Give me not up to the will of my adversaries.*" Physical and spiritual enemies are hard to ignore. All the onslaughts of life and the troubles that surge in upon us constantly weigh heavy on us. He finished his Psalm with the confident declaration that the Lord's goodness, not David's enemies, would engulf his life. He would not be overwhelmed by the enemy. Tough circumstances could not overcome him. He was safe in the Lord. He would endure and experience life along with those around him "*in the land of the living*".

His final word is a challenge to all: "*wait for the Lord*". "*Wait*" is a word commending faith and enduring trust in the goodness of God. Implicit in this word to wait is the idea that seeking the presence of the Lord and learning to delight in his beauty is a lengthy process. One grows into it by patient asking and waiting.

33.
SATISFACTION – DISSATISFACTION, Psalm 63:1-8

A Psalm of David, when he was in the wilderness of Judah.

"O God, you are my God; earnestly I seek you; my soul thirsts for you; my flesh faints for you, as in a dry and weary land where there is no water.

So I have looked upon you in the sanctuary, beholding your power and glory.

Because your steadfast love is better than life, my lips will praise you.

So I will bless you as long as I live; in your name I will lift up my hands.

My soul will be satisfied as with fat and rich food, and my mouth will praise you with joyful lips,

when I remember you upon my bed, and meditate on you in the watches of the night;

for you have been my help, and in the shadow of your wings I will sing for joy.

My soul clings to you; your right hand upholds me."

In Psalm 63, David was consumed with both a hunger for God, and yet paradoxically, a deep satisfaction and joy. The passage drips with a wanting, wanting more than he has: *"O God, earnestly and early I seek you; my soul thirsts for you; my flesh faints for you..."* Eugene Peterson, in his version The

Message, accurately puts it, *"O God, I can't get enough of you!"* It is obvious that David didn't have enough of God to satisfy his soul.

Day after day this burning thirst for God demanded his attention. He couldn't get away from it. It drove him. In fact, every day the thirst hit him early. The Hebrew word for "earnestly" in vs. 1 also carries the idea of "early" (which the KJV uses). In other words, when a person is in earnest about something, he is likely to apply himself to it early. So David was saying, "My God, I want you earnestly, and early." Did David find on his first waking instinct that his heart turned toward God? Quite likely. That may have been astounding for David – to realize that his hunger for God captured him immediately at the beginning of the day.

The experience of thirst was a physical reality for David. Wilderness life, where he had been driven from one place to another to escape the murderous intentions of Saul, was not a pleasant existence. Water was scarce. No doubt he went many days with barely enough to drink. A person trekking across those barren wastes would be consumed with the need to find water. He would look constantly in wadis and ravines for it. His body would incessantly remind him of his desperate need.

David found himself walking through a spiritual wilderness where the "water of God" was not enough. It might appear that David would continue his quest in a negative spirit: "I can't get enough...". He could have written with more of a moaning, complaining voice. Quite often when a person has not gotten enough of what he wants, he complains. The opposite was true with David. He wrote a Psalm full of rejoicing and praise. In fact, it seems that the height of his praise is matched by the depth of his discontent. He actually spoke of being satisfied with God as one who satiates himself with rich food, one who feasts at the most elaborate banquet with the greatest of delicacies. Just thinking about God, and meditating on him, filled David with praise (vs 5-6). Nights can be long, especially if one is in a wilderness, physically or spiritually. But David's nights were a spiritual feast. Thoughts of God filled his soul with delight.

Another paradox of Scripture presents itself: how can a person be dissatisfied with his status – longing for more of God – and yet experience a deep, abiding satisfaction, to the point of joyfulness, with what he already has in God? How could David say, *"My soul thirsts for you"* and at the same time *"Your steadfast love is better than life"* (vs 3)? Or, "God, I'm not content with what I have in you, but to be an object of your love is better than anything my life can offer"? How can he say, *"My flesh faints for you"*, on the one hand, and yet, on the other, *"In the shadow of your wings I sing for joy"*?

The thirst for God that David experienced must be generated by God himself. God wants his people to want him. He wants them to experience him more and more. And an experience with God will create a desire for more, an automatic discontent. It will create a satisfaction of the soul that makes it cry out for greater and greater exposure to God. God satisfies our soul, then he pulls us deeper into relationship with him. David was explicit about this: *"You open your hand and satisfy the desires of every living thing"* (Ps 145:16). And also: *"He satisfies you with good, so that your youth is renewed like the eagle's"* (Ps 103:5). It parallels the nature of love which we characterize as "infatuation" (a weak definition of what is actually pure eros love). Two people in love can't get enough of each other. Each one's soul hungers for more of the other person. This dynamic energizes the drama of the Song of Solomon. As we read the poem, we can see that the Lover and Beloved can't say enough beautiful words about each other. Each is consumed with longing for the other as well as having a joy in each other. A fruitful habit is to ask myself frequently, "What do I really, really want?" I may not get a clear answer. But I can ask God to reveal to me the desires that dwell in my heart. When he shows me, I can present those to him. He will satisfy my desires in his way and his time.

David was really describing a love relationship with God and God with him: "My God, I love you so much. I can't contain my joy. I want you more and more. It's a spiritual thirst within me. And you have shown me that your love for me, better than life itself, draws me toward you like a magnet. I cannot conceive of turning away from that. I don't ever want to because it's plain that you want me, hungering and thirsting for me, far more than I can ever do for you. As you spread your protective wings over me, my soul bubbles over with joy."

"For the mountains may depart
and the hills be removed,
but my steadfast love
will not depart from you..."
Isaiah 54:10

34.
WAITING FOR A REBEL
(Luke 15:11-24)

He sat quietly in his inner room, in semi-darkness. Alone. We don't know his name. His lips moved but no words were heard. His heart was heavy, his spirit crushed. The events of the day before still felt like sword thrusts. His memory only increased the hurt. Where had he failed? How could his youngest son treat him like this? He had been here for these many years, and now he was gone. Finally, words spilled forth.

> "Lord God above, hear my plea. My heart is weighted down with grief. With sorrow. That which I never expected has come upon me. By your command, you directed us to teach our children to walk in your ways, to obey the law, to do right. Faithfully, I trained my sons diligently in that manner. I talked of you as we walked to the fields, as we sat at meals in the house, as I bid them good night. They were respectful of all I said."

"My Child, I know you and I know him. I raised you up to be my own. You have faithfully practiced righteousness, in your own conduct and in what you have taught your sons. You are a prized person of Israel, and precious to me. As is your son. I have loved him as I have loved you with my deep insistent love. I have watched him grow up healthy and strong. He loved life and was full of adventure. He was so tuned in to the world around him, wanting to taste all that this world could offer. He was what I always envisioned sons should be."

"And yet, God of my fathers, why would my son despise me and your law by asking for his inheritance now, before his older brother gets to claim it? What evil forces have moved him to such an act? He wants to be his own man, to get away from my influence, to be independent. He acts as if my teaching in the law was a huge imposition on him, an affront, disrespecting his personal choices. What could I do but give him his estate and let him go? And now he is gone, gone to I know not where, to do what I am fearful may be harmful to him. He said he wants to pursue pleasures that have been denied him. This is not what he was taught. He knows better. Yet he insisted on his right to determine his own way. It's not how our family structures work. It breaks all traditions. But he doesn't care. He doesn't think of us, his mother who bore him and I who have provided for him. I feel so betrayed. I am hurt beyond description. And the guilt of my failure as a parent weighs on me as an unbearable load. Will I ever see him again? Will he destroy himself? Will he shame our family? Answer me, O Father of all, for I too am a father."

"You did not fail, faithful man of Israel. You need have no guilt in this matter. It was not your actions or words that led him to leave your house. In a sense, he is no longer yours. He is exercising his own will to determine what life will bring to him. And just so you know, this is a necessary part of his training, a part you maybe can't understand right now, a part beyond your control. He left, thinking he was free of your influence. Thinking he was free, free at last from your restraints. But there are many, many things he

does not know about life, and especially about freedom. About grace and forgiveness. About me."

"You did well to let him go, to refrain from harassing or judging him. I understand how hard that is. Do you not recall how I have had to let my wayward people have their own way? Do you think what you feel so deeply is not what I have felt? In fact, dear father, your son's conduct hurts me as well. I grieve for him, and with you. I have always sorrowed when my people have rebelled."

"It is natural to wonder if he will hurt himself. Your love for him is bound-less. I do not share those fears, of course, knowing the future as I do. However, you asked me for answers. What I cannot tell you is what you most want to know: will he be all right? Will he follow my laws? Will he come back? Will he come to faith again? But let me ask you this: are you willing to wait? To be patient? You have let him go in a physical sense. Can you let him go in your heart? I know that's not possible in one sense, but in another sense you can. Not disowning him as your son! You are not capable of doing that. I mean letting him go into my hands. Not claiming any control or insisting on any outcomes. I know how to handle your son. He is no match for me. In fact, when someone challenges my right to their life, I find pleasure in taking up that challenge. I have infinite ways of reaching into a person's soul to make them aware of what reality is."

"If you can wait, and I will give you strength to do that, can you wait in kindness? With a forgiving spirit? If you can do that, you will be expressing what I myself am like in a way that mere words cannot. My deep insistent love knows no limits. And I am kind, beyond what anyone can imagine. So, I ask you to present yourself as I have been doing toward my people for genera-tions. I ask you to wait with patient loving and kind expectation. Dear father, this story was not over when your son walked out the door and broke your heart. There is more, much more. And let me encourage you to hope, for I am able to do more than you ask or think. With that in mind, do what your heart now guides you to do."

He praised his Lord God. He sat quietly for yet a while. Then he went out, walked to the end of the path leading up to his house. There, as his heart throbbed with kindness and love and forgiveness, he waited. And every day he did the same.

35.
SINGING NATURE

Job's three friends wore themselves out chiding him for his theological ignorance. And Job himself was exhausted in contradicting them. Then a fourth character, Elihu, attempted to interpret Job's plight to him. He could explain what God was doing! Finally, God himself broke into the drama and challenged Job with penetrating questions: "Where were you when I laid the foundation of the earth? Tell me, if you have understanding...., or who laid its cornerstone, *when the morning stars sang together* and all the sons of God shouted for joy?" (Job 38:7 emphasis added).

Morning stars singing? Venus pouring forth a melody at the dawning of the day? Jupiter humming? How shall we assess language like this? The excessive imaginations of a poetic mind? Just fanciful visions having no basis in reality? Just literary license? Was something happening at the creation that is no longer in effect? Can any of us claim to have heard such music?

A passing allusion to singing stars may not seem to carry much theological weight. However, many insights flash across the screen of God's Word, begging to be explored further. And one finds in pursuing some of those insights further that a whole new perspective opens up. Our lives are enriched by new treasures.

Thus, in examining some of the more poetic parts of Scripture, we catch a glimpse of hidden truths. Is there music out there we are not hearing? Perhaps it's helpful to establish first God has a love for music. Heaven seems to be a very musical place. The atmosphere in the dwelling place of God appears to throb with melody and harmony. Angels sing, we learn from Revelation 5. So maybe it's not surprising that God pulls back the veil a bit, telling us of singing stars and dancing mountains.

Even science reflects on the music of a natural world. The Greek mathematician Pythagoras said, "...the principles of triangles were just a single note in the grand musical work that was the cosmos..." Mark Ballora in "Sound: The Music of the Universe", (February 23, 2013) wrote, "Today, we may think of the Music of the Spheres as being more fanciful than scientific. Yet musical language appears frequently in astronomers' descriptions of space…. The more we learn about the universe, the more we seem to rely on musical terminology to describe it." Other astrophysicists talk more and more of the sounds heavenly bodies emit. Honor Harger said in the Huffington Post, "Tuning Into The Universe" (February 24, 2013): "The sounds of Jovian moons Ganymede , Europa and Callisto are amongst the most musical of the recordings we have encountered….We can listen to the Sun's fizzling solar flares, the roaring waves and spitting fire of Jupiter's stormy interactions with its moon Io, pulsars' metronomic beats, or the eerie melodic shimmer of a whistler in the magnetosphere."

Dennis Overbye, wrote in the New York Times (Sept. 16 2003), "Astronomers say they have heard the sound of a black hole singing. And what it is singing, perhaps…for more than two billion years…is B flat – a B flat 57 octaves lower than middle C…. The black hole is playing 'the lowest note in the universe,' said Dr. Andrew Fabian, an X-ray astronomer at Cambridge, 'The one thing that connects everything in the Universe is music, or sound. Everything and every one of us is energy… and that is vibrating. When things vibrate, they create sound waves, which we hear as music as well as feel.'"

So is it surprising that we find David claiming to hear strains of music coming from the natural world? In Psalm 65, David pictured God attending to Israel's crops, watering the land, stimulating growth. As a result, David said,

> *"The pastures of the wilderness overflow, the hills gird themselves with joy, the meadows clothe themselves with flocks, the*

valleys deck themselves with grain, they shout and sing together for joy" (vs. 12).

And in Psalm 96 an unknown Psalmist wrote,

"Let the heavens be glad, and let the earth rejoice; let the sea roar, and all that fills it; let the field exult, and everything in it! Then shall all the trees of the forest sing for joy..." (vss. 11-12).

Those verses run parallel to the same theme in Psalm 98, again by an anonymous writer:

"Make a joyful noise to the LORD, all the earth; break forth into joyous song and sing praises!... Let the sea roar, and all that fills it; the world and those who dwell in it! Let the rivers clap their hands; let the hills sing for joy together..." (vss. 4, 7-8).

This Psalmist celebrated the salvation the Lord promised to bring to the world, along with his righteous rule. And in the Spirit, the writer saw that all creation was enraptured at what their Lord is doing for the people he loves. It is interesting that Isaac Watts, that great hymn writer of the 18th century, used that Psalm and that theme to write "Joy to the World". It has become well-entrenched as a Christmas hymn, but its original intent was to magnify the glory of Christ and his salvation:

"Joy to the world, the Lord has come
Let earth receive her King
Let every heart prepare Him room
And Heaven and nature sing

And Heaven and nature sing

And Heaven, and Heaven, and nature sing
Joy to the world, the Savior reigns!

Let men their songs employ
While fields and floods, rocks, hills and plains
Repeat the sounding joy
Repeat the sounding joy."

And the author of Psalm 148:3-4, quite likely David again, visualized musical praise when he calls on all creation to praise the Lord:

"Praise him, sun and moon, praise him, all you shining stars! Praise him, you highest heavens, and you waters above the heavens!...Praise the LORD...you great sea creatures and all deeps, fire and hail, snow and mist, stormy wind fulfilling his word! Mountains and all hills, fruit trees and all cedars! Beasts and all creeping things and flying birds!"

When praise is called forth, the Old Testament writers usually associated music with the act of praising. When David wrote: *"All your works shall give thanks to you, O LORD..."* (Psalm 145:10), did he not envision all of God's works bursting forth in grateful song?

David clearly thought of creation as having a message. His metaphoric lines in Psalm 19 present the heavens as declaring God's glory. *"Day to day pours out speech, and night to night reveals knowledge,"* David said (vs.2). When tied to other scriptures that picture nature, and the universe in particular as pouring out praise in song, we can believe David thought speech issuing from the heavens was praiseful, musical speech.

Modern song writers picked up on this theme from Psalm 19. Steve Green, in an album from 1989, sang:

"All creation has a language
Words to say what must be said
All day long the heavens whisper...

'God is glorious, perfect, light...'
All creation sings his praises

Earth and heaven praise his name
All who live come join the chorus
Find the words his love proclaim."

But a vision of nature in song is not limited to the poetic David. The prophet Isaiah also imagined a praiseful natural world:

"Sing, O heavens, for the LORD has done it; shout, O depths of the earth; break forth into singing, O mountains, O forest, and every tree in it! For the LORD has redeemed Jacob, and will be glorified in Israel" (Isa 44:33).

"Sing for joy, O heavens, and exult, O earth; break forth, O mountains, into singing! For the LORD has comforted his people and will have compassion on his afflicted" (Isa 49:13).

"For you shall go out in joy and be led forth in peace; the mountains and the hills before you shall break forth into singing, and all the trees of the field shall clap their hands" (Isa 55:12).

Isaiah celebrated the wonder of God's restoration of his exiled people to their land, both in Isaiah's relatively near future, but also in the ultimate end of time victory they would enjoy. And he cannot help but think all creation rejoiced as well.

As was mentioned above, the images in the last book of the Bible reinforce what Old Testament writers pictured for us. In Revelation, when John was in the Spirit and caught up before the throne of God, he was given visions of reality not immediately available to us in our earth-bound minds. Living creatures and twenty-four elders rejoiced over the presentation of, Jesus, the Lamb of God slain for our redemption. They sing a new song of Christ's worthiness. From there, John is overwhelmed with literally millions of angels rejoicing together and also declaring, with musical praise implied, the worthiness of the Lamb. And finally, John is presented with a crescendo of praise, where *"every creature in heaven and on earth"* joins the chorus, giving highest honor and esteem to *"him who sits on the throne and to the Lamb"* (Rev 5:9-13). The image is of a natural world, every part of it, uttering praise to God and the Lord Jesus Christ. That praise is an echo of the musical atmosphere of heaven. Music appears to be the language of our soul and of all creation because it is the breath of life around the throne of God.

So how are we to understand these seemingly fanciful statements? Our natural bent is to interpret Scripture very literally. And we tend to be wary of figurative language because, of course, the imagination can lead us into wild speculations. Indeed, in past history, allegorizing of Scripture led readers into fantasy land, seemingly with no limit to the author's imagination.

But is there some reality here? Do trees actually celebrate, clapping their hands? Do mountains sing? Or were the biblical writers overly enamored of poetic expression, language we might dismiss as purely imaginative? Were they simply excited by metaphoric language? Or might it be possible that one needs a special faculty to apprehend the music of the world? Can some people grasp that phenomenon better than others? Even Jesus seemed aware of this, implying that natural materials had the energy of praise locked up within them. On his descent from the Mount of Olives, Jesus' disciples were praising God, probably in song, and rejoicing at the amazing things they had seen. Some Pharisees told Jesus to silence his disciples, whereupon Jesus said, *"If these were silent, the very stones would cry out"* (Luke 19:37-40). Stones poised to express pent-up praise?

Was it not Friedrich Nietzsche who recognized that some people could apprehend truths that others completely missed: "And those who were seen dancing were thought to be insane by those who could not hear the music"? Paul wrote *"we see through a glass darkly"* (1 Corinthians 13:12). Indeed, we do when it comes to grasping what may well be an aspect of nature expressed in Scripture. It is true we do not hear mountains singing or trees clapping their hands with our natural faculties, so we must conclude there is another way of entering into this biblical "reality".

When Isaiah encountered the Lord in the temple, high and lifted up, he watched and listened in awe as seraphs proclaimed: *"Holy, holy, holy is the Lord God Almighty! The whole earth is full of his glory"* (Isaiah 6:3). Perhaps, with biblical images of a praising creation in mind, we can celebrate that glory in the world. We can simply appreciate the fact that there is a melody of praise occurring in a world that sings and claps in ways we cannot fully comprehend. With majestic mountains in view, we can, in spirit, join in their song of praise. A walk in a forest land can draw us into its applause of the glory of God. Observing the heavens on a darkened night can find us resonating with their grand chorus of worship, as they radiate an ovation to the God who created them. As the ocean roars and pounds in front of us, we listen for the song exalting the Lord God. And so, in all we encounter in our world – billowing clouds, delicate blossoms, the glistening dew, a vast expanse of sandy beach, thundering waterfalls, far-flung grasslands – our souls can rejoice in the melody of creation in which we will someday be full participants.

"This is my Father's world,
And to my listening ears,
All nature sings and round me rings,
The music of the spheres."

If music is truly the language of the soul, as we can imagine it is, and nature makes music, there are implications for eternity. All creation cries to God in the language of the soul and God joins in its melody. And that language is brought into eternity by every living thing, where all will join in one magnificent song to Christ Jesus our Lord.

36.
SORROW AS NO OTHER

"Look and see if there is any sorrow like my sorrow, which was brought upon me..." (Lamentations 1:12).

A lonesome man stands on a street corner in ancient Jerusalem in the year 586 B. C. His eyes take in the scene around him, one of awful devastation. He can see the smoke of fires rising from far off in the center of the city! And woe of woes – the temple is on fire! God's dwelling place among his people! Burning, burning, burning! It cannot be! How can God allow a barbarian people, the Babylonians, to desecrate and destroy such a sacred place? And, not satisfied with burning God's holy place, they are leveling the walls of the city. Huge blocks of stone are being toppled, one after another. Houses around him have been razed, their possessions ransacked by drunken soldiers. Majestic palaces of leading citizens are in ruins, their owners pierced through with the sword.

His heart recoils at the scene of bodies stacked up in the streets nearby, adults and children. Some drip blood from spear and sword wounds, others are blackened and bloated by the starvation that has gripped the city, their skin tight on protruding bones. He can hear the plaintive cries of babies, craving their mothers' breasts, to no avail. Two years of siege by the Babylonian army has finally brought the city to capitulation. But not before horrific things had been done in his beloved city. Residents have become so desperate for food that some have boiled and eaten their own children. And now wives and daughters have been raped. Holy men tortured and slaughtered.

It should not be! This city, the very possession of God, cannot be destroyed. Did not the prophets and priests tell him that the city could never be vanquished? God would defend his precious jewel. Where is his God? Why has he forsaken them? Does he not love them anymore?

Grief breaks his heart. He experiences what appears to be the total destruction of his whole world, and he simply cannot comprehend it. His question arises out of the wrenching of his inner being: *"Look, you who pass by...Is there any sorrow like my sorrow?"* (Lam. 1"12).

All those who have ever grieved may have posed the same question, be it from the death of a loved one, the loss of something or someone precious, the breakup of a relationship. Their pain seems to be so much greater than anyone else's pain. How can anyone else understand the depth of their sorrow? It feels so unique, so personal, so individual. They readily dismiss anyone saying, "Oh, I understand your pain." It is felt those others can't possibly know the nature of such grief and loss. Grief is intensified when one cannot even share the loss that grips one's heart.

Countless people have suffered and sorrowed over the centuries. Grief is old; it is not new at all. One could look at a sufferer and with insensitive spirit say, "Get over it. Lots of people have gone through what you have experienced." But it's misguided direction. For the writer observing the ruinous scene of Jerusalem knows in his heart of hearts that everyone's grief is their own. In a real sense, no one can enter into someone else's sorrow. It is too unique, too individual. It is one's own, and no one but God can penetrate the heart of sorrow and identify fully with it. There is some truth to the fact that each person must suffer alone and in silence. Every sorrowing person says in some way, "Look and see, is there really any sorrow like my sorrow? No, no one has experienced this pain as I am experiencing it now. No one can understand what this loss means to me." Even the writer of Proverbs acknowledges that no one can enter fully into someone else's sorrow: *"The heart knows its own bitterness, and no stranger shares its joy"* (14:10).

But the word of Scripture is that there is One who has. He has *"...borne our griefs and carried our sorrows..."* (Isaiah 53:4). And the Psalmist reinforces that truth with the claim: *"The Lord is near to the brokenhearted and saves the crushed in spirit"* (Psalm 34:18). Our abiding consolation is that our God understands the pain of our hearts more fully than we ourselves do.

And more than anyone else can. The Psalmist addresses the Lord, *"When the cares [sorrows] of my heart are many, your consolations cheer my soul"* (Psalm 94:19).

Interestingly, the Lord employs "angel helpers" in sending his comfort and cheer into a sorrowing heart. He challenges his followers to come alongside a grieving person and encourage them. He points out through the apostle Paul that God is a God of comfort who comforts us in all our affliction (2 Cor 1:3-4). As he comforts us, our Father wants the Body of Christ to be his servants in comforting others. *"...weep with those who weep"* (Romans 12:15). Though it is true no one can fully appreciate another's sorrow, it is a source of comfort when someone with wise understanding can walk partway with a grieving soul. They don't have to say much, or try to diminish another's sorrow. Clichés and platitudes work no magic. But caring has magic in itself. And presence has power to dissipate pain, slowly and gradually.

Life has few roles more compelling than fellow believers in Jesus administering his deep compassions, especially to those who feel they sorrow as no one else sorrows.

37.

VIEWING SUMMER CLOUDS WITH THE TOP DOWN

(in my little VW Beetle convertible)

Summer clouds. Are they not unique?
Cotton balls on high, fluffy, puffy and plumpish.
Not the gray clouds of winter, blanketing the sky.
So individual, unattached, floating high above me,
     beholden to no one.
Right there above my head, can I touch them?

Drifting lonely, lonely and quiet, quiet and aimless.
Where are they going? Where did they come from?
Who directs their paths?
Will they collide? How do they stay up there?
Why don't they fall?
Can we ride on a horse-shaped cloud?

Just drift along wherever it's going, carefree,
exulting over all things below?

Who sculptures these splotches of the heavens?
Amorphous tops and with carved-flat bottoms.
Just formless, random shapes.

But look, there's a bunny floating by!
And over there an elephant!
There's a dog, ears pointing skyward!
And there, there to the south, a duck!
How exciting – pictures in the sky!
Will you lay in a meadow and imagine shapes,
And then argue about them
Till shapes morph back again to simple blobs?
See who finds a butterfly?
Who sees the most shapes?

Alone they float, till they pass from view.
Alone they drift, slowly merging into larger mass;
They merge and merge till one single cloud towers high,
Thrusting itself up, up and up till winds whip its top apart
And thunderheads loom nearer and nearer.

Summer clouds! Majestic gifts,
Gifts from the One who loves clouds!

38.
Summer Longings

The smell of summer evening draws a sigh,
enhanced by cotton-candy sky.
Where is that slinking moon in pastel cloud?
Ruling the night, head unbowed?
Joyful, warmish wind, caress my face,
Tussle my hair, all out of place.
How can I store this gift forever?
Hold in my hand, releasing never?
Wonderfully joyous, wonderfully sad!
Foretaste of heaven to be had!

39.

A Lovely Place to Dwell - PSALM 84

The traveler made his way to Jerusalem. Up to Jerusalem. Going to the City of God was always up, no matter from what direction a traveler came. He was on a mission – to worship God at the temple, the magnificent structure built by King Solomon. Generations of Israelites had made this trek. It was always a moving experience. They came from the countryside to Jerusalem, the very heart of Jewish life.

As he drew near to the city, from the heights around it, the traveler could look down on that splendid edifice, the temple. He exclaimed as he watched, *"How lovely is your dwelling place, O LORD of hosts!"* (vs. 1) The longing which had built up throughout his journey now burst forth in a bold word to his God: *"My soul longs, yes, faints for the courts of the LORD; my heart and flesh sing for joy to the living God"* (vs. 2). The anticipation of meeting the Lord God in temple worship almost overwhelmed our traveler. He loved God. He yearned to praise God.

The traveler passed through the Eastern Gate into the Outer Courtyard, the major gathering place for worshipers. Levites and priests moved about, fulfilling their commission by God to maintain temple worship. How fortunate they were to spend the whole of their lives in the dwelling place of God. The traveler envied them: *"Blessed are those who dwell in your house, ever singing your praise!"* (vs. 4). As he looked around further, he spotted birds flitting here and there among the columns of stone. And amazingly, some were nesting close to the altar! The Lord even welcomed birds into his house. The traveler voiced his astonishment, *"Even the sparrow finds a home, and the swallow a nest for herself, where she may lay her young, at your altars, O LORD of hosts, my King and my God!"* (vs. 3). How blessed were the lowly birds! Their instinct drew them to a place of worship.

The traveler was weary from his long journey. He sat on a temple bench to rest as he thought back on his pilgrimage. He reflected on the countless other Israelites still on the roads, on their pilgrimage to Jerusalem. It struck him that these would-be worshipers were already blessed by God by reason of their intentions: *"Blessed are those whose strength is in you, in whose heart are the highways to Zion"* (vs. 5). They too were in earnest about meeting God in his sanctuary. Their desire to go to the temple had been of the Lord's promptings. They knew he promised to be their protecting strength on the way.

The journey had been arduous, and long. Many hills had to be ascended. If one were a solitary traveler, the valleys held a fearsome possibility. Assaults were not unknown. Marauding bandits posed a real threat. One valley in particular had been labeled the Valley of Baca, which meant "weeping". The traveler had heard of some who had been robbed and beaten there, left weeping and bereft. But he and his fellow travelers had determined not to let Baca be a weeping experience. The springs crossing the valley path spoke to them of the life-giving resource of their God. The prospect of meeting God in Zion was exhilarating: *"As they go through the Valley of Baca, they make it a place of springs; the early rain also covers it with pools"* (vs. 6). Instead of anguished weeping, happy tears had streamed down his face. He had found the water refreshing as he dipped from rushing streams. Life-giving water quenched the thirst generated by the hot, dusty trek through the hills.

As the traveler reflected further on his journey, he remembered those who advised against it. They had warned about robbers, but also that one's enthusiasm for the venture would wane. Everyone knew it required endurance to accomplish their goal. As he rested, the worshiper was amazed at how refreshed he was. It was the Lord. He had enabled him to *"...go from strength to strength; each one* [who] *appeared before God in Zion"* (vs. 7). This man was blessed to know it was God himself who energized those who pursued him. Not surprisingly, he blurted out, *"O LORD God of hosts, hear my prayer; give ear, O God of Jacob!"* (vs. 8). And he thought too of the king: *"Behold our shield, O God; look on the face of your anointed!"* (vs. 9). O that God would bless the anointed King to lead his people.

The hustle and bustle of the temple grounds caught the worshiper's eye. Priests and Levites mingled with worshipers, performing the sacrificial rituals. What a privilege it must be to work right here in God's special meeting place! Oh, just to remain here forever! He couldn't help but exclaim to God: *"...a day in your courts is better than a thousand elsewhere"* (vs. 10). He couldn't be a priest or Levite. They were especially ordained of God for temple service. But what about a doorkeeper? He had noticed them as he entered the temple grounds. He would gladly stoop to that role if possible. Yes, his heart said to him, *"I would rather be a doorkeeper in the house of my God than dwell in the tents of wickedness"* (vs. 10).

Sitting in the heat of the sun, this faithful worshipper could only conclude that great blessing came to the person who trusted God to overshadow his life with all he needed – a "shade" from the burning sun and yet a welcome "sun" to light a dark day: *"For the LORD God is a sun and shield; the LORD bestows favor and honor"* (vs. 11). God's very nature exuded favor to those who made the effort to meet him. For the traveler, just to be here at the temple was a joy itself. His God had been full of compassion toward him as he thought further: *"No good thing does he withhold from those who walk uprightly. O LORD of hosts, blessed is the one who trusts in you!"* (vs. 11-12).

The picture of a traveler coursing his way to Jerusalem to meet his God can be a metaphor for anyone earnestly seeking God, even without a geographic location. If I set myself up to come before God I will find, as the Psalmist-traveler did, that the way can be wearying and distractions arise. Strength can wane and willpower may fade. Along the way occasions of weeping are inevitable. But the contemporary "worshiper-seeker" will find the Psalmist's God bestowing favor, reinvigorating the weary, comforting the mournful, refreshing the needy. And I will discover, as did the Psalmist-traveler, that I may want more than anything to remain in the presence of the Lord and become passionate about serving him. The Psalmist's threefold experience of blessing can be ours: the blessing of being in the place where God dwells, the blessing of finding God to be our strength for the journey, and the blessing of simply entrusting one's life to Him who comes to meet us too.

40.
THE DOOR

In every life there stands a door,
                a closed door,
           locked from the other side.
     An unseen door, yet always there,
             its presence dim, its meaning veiled,
      yet haunting each man's soul.
                What does it hide?
    Past the door each life proceeds,
            day by day,
                year into year,
       unlooking, unsearching, paying no heed,
    through childhood, and especially youth,
          with reckless deeds
              that thrust them at the door,
              threatening to break through.

Croup and pox and fever in the night
find loved ones grim,
pleading with One to guard the door,
then thankful, happy to find it closed.

For others, Death's door opens, early or late;
Countless others, most unready;
Some passing gently, softly;
Some crashing through with fear-filled eyes
and scream-curled lips,
protesting every step.
Others, always others,
and yet, not me, not me,
not yet!

With added years the door looms nearer, larger.
Life's paths draw closer,
though not with dread.
New questions rise:
"Who waits beyond the door?"
"What realness can be known there?"
"Who rules that unseen world?"
"Sooner...or later, will one enter?"
Days pass more quickly, seemingly endless,
And life's unnumbered acts draw one steadily nearer,
nearer the door.
Then,
one day,
suddenly,
the door stands ajar,
and life's path curves close toward its darkened frame.
Panic rules:
"Oh no! Not me!
"Oh no! Not now!"
Reluctance drags the feet, resisting the current,

fighting back, back from the door,
groping for another path, finding none.
And sadness saturates the soul
for all that must be let go…
…of family joys,
…of simple pleasures,
…of life's long labors
crowned with due reward,
…of friendships dear and deep;
A letting-go, surrendering a myriad of precious things.

New questions mount, intensely so;
The soul pouring forth prayers and tears,
emitting anguished pleas.
Mystery floods the mind,
Pain's heartless grip confounds the will.
This captivating 'Thing', this destroyer of all good,
this unrelenting foe,
it <u>will</u> <u>not</u> let go,
tugging one closer, closer to that unknown threshold.

Then **Truth** begins its soft advance…
…commanding **Hope**
to claim the **realness** of all that's been
taught
and lived
and first believed;
to confirm the Word of One who Himself
passed through the door,
tasting its bitter cup for everyone;
…calling Peace to whisper:
"In spite of all, all will be well;"
…inviting Joy
to temper pain,
to overlay grief with gladness

for all that was given of life and love;

...directing Faith

to grant new sight to see,

to see Him

whose presence grows more clearly now,

His wounded sides and hands more visible;

to view Him standing by the door,

ushering in all who come to Him;

to hear His voice of reassuring power:

"Don't be afraid; I will be with you!

There is joy, full joy...

There is life, real life...

There's a home, a ready home...

And it is better, far better...

...beyond the door,

where some day doors will be no more!"

So the door swings open wide,

And then comes the last great letting-go!

Silently one passes through.

Slowly, quietly it shuts again,

While others watch and weep and wonder.

They too have a door,

made more desirable

because of him who now

LIVES

on the other side!

41.
THE MOON

Like a jewel of the morn,
the moon soars on high,
flaunting its beauty,
God's grace in the sky.

Kept in its orbit
by earth's steady tug.
So, we, embraced in the circle
of God's ne'er-ending hug.

42.
THE RUSH OF SILENCE

Can you hear the silence?
Here on this woodsy path?
As moonlight streams through yellow leaves?

Stop! Listen!
You can hear it,
A quietness falling with the dew,
Creeping,
        seeping,
Past white-stalked birch and darkened pine,
Caressing red-tinged maple.

Stop! Don't move!
Leaf-crunching footsteps
Undo the stillness.
Once rustling leaves refuse to quake,
Awed by the wonder of a silent woods.

Stop! Don't speak!
No words enrich
The calmness of the night.
No speech can gild the hush around you.

The silence! The quiet!
It embraces, it dazes you!

Its thunder trembles you!
Its stillness floods your heart!
Oh, listen to the silence of the sacred woods!

43.
WALKING

I walked one morning up into the high hills above Palm Springs, CA. It was on a favorite trail that I have hiked in past visits there. The path ascended from just off a main roadway, E. Palm Canyon, up and up to the San Jacinto range. These trails would lead a person far into the hills, ascending to 4,000 or 5,000 feet. My climb was very modest, in all maybe 500 feet vertically, according to my GPS app on my phone. And at my age, it was a slower hike than some who passed me by, like the man who ran up the slope this morning. He looked so fit!

The path was mostly scraped out of the mountainside long ago by bulldozers. But the eroding effects of rain had sculpted the surface in ways that require careful walking. I looked down a lot, watching where my feet had to go. That's unfortunate because in so doing, I missed observing the land around me. It's not possible to walk safely with head held high, savoring the air and sky. The same holds true when I have walked the paths of a forest. Tree roots and the like created the same risk of stumbling and tripping.

It is only by the actual experience of walking that a person can glean what biblical authors and speakers were attempting to teach in various passages. They use the metaphor of physical walking to call forth spiritual principles and truths. People of Palestine and the Mediterranean area walked. They walked here; they walked there. They were always coming from somewhere on foot, and going somewhere on foot. They walked and walked and walked. They walked uphill. They walked downhill. Knowing the terrain of Palestine, it can be said safely that they hardly ever walked a level pathway. Not surprisingly, King David asks God to lead him on a level path (Psalm 27:4). It was the Roman road engineers who eventually leveled hills and valleys, somewhat. Maybe the Pax Romana referred not so much to cessation of war as it did to the quieting of travelers' complaints about all the ups and downs of walking!

We know Jesus walked the roadways and trails into the hills of Judea and Galilee. We know Paul trekked immense distances on his church building missions. Most interesting would be to know how many pairs of sandals they wore out. A sandal-maker in Palestine must have had a booming business.

The writers and speakers of the first century used the word "walk" to indicate a course of life, a manner or way of life. Thus, "walk" basically described a person's life as it transpired, especially the manner in which that life was lived.

138

Paul, Jesus, John and Jude all projected this picture of walking. It was so natural to them. Walking meant going somewhere, moving forward, reaching destinations. Walkers were movers. They faced forward, going yonder to someplace ahead. No one deliberately walked backwards.

The slow business of walking also called for patience. How can our culture appreciate the patience of walking, physically or spiritually, when we are so addicted to faster and faster? If we could master the science, we would want instant arrivals, with no irritating time gap between departure and destination. I read long ago, when air travel was just becoming prevalent, of an executive who flew from Los Angeles to New York. He exclaimed disgustedly on landing, "Five hours to New York! I could have walked that fast!" Even then air travel was generating an impatience that a first century person would have found astounding.

Just like a physical walk, a spiritual walk required patience too. Hard going uphill? Just keep putting one foot in front of the other. I experienced that dramatically while on a hike to the 14,600 foot peak of Mount Harvard in Colorado. My pace, as I neared the top, was agonizingly slow. Literally, one step more, then another, one foot in front of the other. Patience. Such as is needed in the walk we are called to with Christ.

One can sense the intentionality in biblical writers' use of the word "walk". They found it a perfect metaphor for a Christian life. Life was a journey. Believers, disciples, were meant to be moving, traveling from one point to another. Facing forward, not back. "I have decided to follow (walk after) Jesus, no turning back...", goes the little chorus. Progression, not regression, fit so beautifully with the walking image. Paul spoke of *"forgetting what lies behind and straining for what lies ahead"* (Phil. 3:13). Onward, onward, ever onward. Both Jesus and Paul spoke of finishing a course (Luke 13:32; Acts 20:24; 2 Tim 4:7, more as a race).

Jesus told his disciples to *"Walk while you have the light..."* (John 12:35), and that if they followed him, they would *"not walk in darkness"* (John 12:35). Maybe it was obscure to his listeners, but he had just claimed: *"I am the light of the world..."* (John 8:12). In the course of their lives, by following him, they would have the *"light of life"* (John 8:12). Light to guide their walk through life. Many a Palestinian knew with what trepidation they had walked paths and roadways in the dark. How wonderful it would be to have a never-ending beam lighting the way! What about life in general, Jesus asks? Do you want never-ending guidance for a safe and satisfying life? You can have it in me.

Paul wrote the most extensively of this picture of walking: Walk in newness of life. We walk by faith and not by sight. Walk by the Spirit. Walk worthy of your calling. Walk in love. Walk carefully, not as unwise, but as wise. Walk worthy of the Lord. He said our pre-Christ life was a walk in the passions of our flesh. And to the Colossians, he said we must put to death those traits in which we once walked. If we offend a brother, we were no longer walking in love. To Paul's insightful mind, the Christian walking journey modeled that of Christ: *"As you have therefore received Christ Jesus as Lord, walk in him"* (Col. 2:6). The apostle John echoed the same: *"Whoever says he abides in [Christ] ought to walk in the same way in which he walked"* 1 John 2:6).

But how does one savor life while walking, especially over rugged uneven terrain? On the journey, moving forward, must we always have our heads down, analyzing where we are going, fearful of tripping and falling? King David was of course greatly familiar with the rugged paths of Judah. He must have been a champion walker. But he recognized the perils of walking, perhaps stumbling and injuring oneself. So, he appealed to the God who made his feet and legs. He recognized that in his life journey, God himself undertakes to prevent our stumbling: *"You gave a wide place for my steps under me, and my feet did not slip"* (Psalm 18:36). And, *"For you have delivered my...feet from stumbling"* (Psalm 116:8).

The God who sets us on a walking journey over both rough and smooth paths is the God who gives us endurance to reach the destination, who secures our steps under us, who indeed walks with us.

44.
WHEN I AWAKE -
Psalm 139:17-18

Our relationship with God harbors mysteries. We cannot explain so many aspects of who God is, what he does and what he thinks. When it comes to a question of what God thinks, the Psalmist David offered some fascinating insights. What does God think of? Confidently, David answered, "God thinks of me!" He wrote, *"How precious to me are your thoughts, O God. How vast is the sum of them. If I could count them, they are more than the sand. And when I awake, I am still with you"* (Psalm 139:17-18). Most versions on this Psalm read *"How precious* to me..." However, the KJV presents us with: *"How precious unto me..."*, where the word "unto" can be interpreted as *"...thoughts of me..."*. One commentator (Matthew Henry) explains the idea as: "God, who knew him, thought of him, and his thoughts towards him were thoughts of love, thought of good, and not of evil."

David considered the number of God's thoughts as more than could be counted. But in the vastness of thoughts which God has, David savored the idea that a great many of those thoughts were about him. God focused his thoughts on David. Those words were written, not just for David to live confidently in this truth, but for all of us who orient ourselves toward God. Likewise, each of us can boldly say, "God thinks about me!" The idea finds reinforcement in what Jesus himself said, *"The very hairs of your head are numbered"* Matthew 10:30). That is, God's focus on me includes knowing every detail of my life.

We may gladly appreciate David's claims regarding the thoughts of God toward us. But David did not end his expression with how incredibly numerous are God's thoughts. He added, *"When I am awake, I am still with you."* Why did David include that last line? What does it have to do with God's thoughts about him? Maybe he was thinking that in sleep he was not really aware of God. That included any sense that God was thinking about him. But when he woke up, immediately, he had an awareness of God. And he can only attribute that to the reality that "God got there first". God was thinking of David before David was thinking of him. In fact, according to the first line of verse 17, David's conclusion was God had not stopped thinking of him at all. Since God's thoughts about him were beyond counting, more than grains of sand on all the ocean shores, he was thinking about David all night long. And, as even as David's sleep dissolves into consciousness, he will not stop thinking of David throughout the day.

At the end of day, when night again brings sleep, and all consciousness fades away, the cycle continues. David was no longer conscious of God. But upon waking, David once again became aware of God's presence: *"When I awake, I am still with you."* And, even more profound and awesome, he was confident that God had again, through the night, been thinking about him, constantly, incessantly!

How marvelous are your works, O Lord!

45.
WHERE IS MY MOTHER?

In 1960, P. D. Eastman penned the classic children's book "Are You My Mother?". The book has sold millions and entertained as many children. I remember reading it to our children. The story presents us with a hatchling bird falling out of the nest, and not finding his mother, sets out on a quest to look for her. The baby bird asks whoever it finds, "Are you my mother?" A kitten, a hen, a dog, a cow, a car, a boat, a plane, and a giant power shovel – all get asked, and the answer is always, "No! I am not your mother!" In the end, the power shovel uses its bucket to drop the hatchling back into its nest, whereupon the mother bird flies back, uniting with her baby.

In essence, the baby bird's cry "Are you my mother?" could have been directed at each object as "Where is my mother?"

I find the question intriguing and totally pertinent. My mother passed away a few years ago, my father a few years before that. The question grips me: "Where is my mother? My father?" They are no longer here. I can't communicate with them, can't visit them, don't receive any word from them. Though memories abound, they have disappeared. They are gone. I cannot buy her a Christmas present, nor will I receive a birthday greeting from her.

Since mankind was turned out of Eden, the question has likewise haunted him. Cultures throughout history and around the globe have had highly developed explanations for what life after death entails. They set forth countless scenarios in trying to answer the question: "Where is my mother? My wife? My husband? My son?". If I were Hindu or Buddhist, the answer might involve an afterlife of endless cycles of death and rebirth. The "soul" would pass through lower realms, learning lessons qualifying a person to advance to higher realms, eventually reaching a nebulous "nirvana", a state of totally suppressed desire. But to those left behind, even if a Buddhist believed there is no soul as such, the same question would still arise, "Where is my mother, my father?".

The memory of one's loved ones remains a powerful force. The quest to know what has happened to them cannot be easily dismissed. Witness Chinese ancestor worship. Practitioners believe they can affect the well-being of ancestors by complex rituals which include shrines in the home. Tablets inscribed with the names and dates of the deceased loved ones can be observed. Food and prayers are offered to the departed daily. The practice of such rituals, and others in various cultures, reinforces the idea of an underlying "where" question of a loved one's existence.

These religions of history and the present world struggle to provide answers. Many have been presented, but none provide absolute assurance of where a loved one is and what is their status. The overwhelming truth is that we have had, and still have, no information from that realm beyond earthly life. Nothing to render proof of where our loved one is. Access into that unseen realm is a closed door.

Job wrestled with this question of afterlife: *"If a man dies, will he live again?"* (Job 14:14). His perspective on one's place after death was limited, typical of the Old Testament view: *"...so a man lies down and rises not again; till the heavens are no more he will not awake or be roused out of his sleep."*

(14:12). Very little revelation enlightened ancient Israelites, yet they too craved understanding of life after death. King David had some further insight: *"As for me, I shall behold your* [God's] *face in righteousness; when I awake, I shall be satisfied with your likeness"* (Psalm 17:15). It could be interpreted that David had an inkling he would in some way be present with the Lord after death. But it was far from a satisfactory picture.

When someone asks, "Where is my mother?", the quick and easy answer for Christians is, "In heaven". But on what basis are they able to make that claim? Would not the claim of a Buddhist be just as valid, that the loved one is absorbed into the All? Who guarantees the validity of an afterlife claim? Not surprisingly, Jesus addressed that nagging question when his friend Lazarus died. Lazarus' sister Martha affirmed her belief he would *"rise again"*. At this, Jesus told her, *"Your brother will rise again. I am the resurrection and the life. Whoever believes in me, though he die, yet shall he live"* (John 11:23, 25). Though not identifying exactly where Lazarus was, Jesus declared there was indeed a place where Lazarus still lived and from which he would be restored to a body. He understood Martha's aching need to know about a loved one's disposition beyond the grave.

The apostle Paul picked up the theme of resurrection in 1 Corinthians 15. No doubt the Corinthian Christians had been asking questions: What happens to our fellow-believers who have "fallen asleep"? Where is my mother? Where is my father? Paul wrote extensively of the resurrection process and outcome. He spoke of heavenly bodies and earthly bodies, natural bodies and spiritual bodies, of first Adams and second Adams. But nowhere did he address the issue of "place": "Where is...?"

It may be Paul was thinking of an incident of years before when he was stoned and left for dead at Lystra. Many Bible teachers believe this was the event Paul referenced in 2 Corinthians 12. He spoke of being caught up to the *"third heaven"*, in *"paradise"* (12:2-3). We read the text, wanting Paul to explain, to elaborate. Just where was this "third heaven"? What did he see there? Who did he see there? Could he have told Barnabas, "I saw your mother there"? Or Martha, "I saw... Lazarus there"? No such message was forthcoming. Instead, we find Paul saying, *"I heard things that cannot be told, which man may not utter"* (vs. 4). So in that discourse, Paul did not give us an answer. We are no closer to knowing. No definitive reference to where one's loved one or friend might be.

A bloodied, beaten man, moments before he died, spoke to Jesus, *"Jesus, remember me when you set up your kingdom"* (Luke 23:42). And Jesus, beaten and bloodied himself, moments before his own death, replied, *"Today you will be with me in paradise"* (Luke 23:43). But, Jesus, where is that? What's it like there? Who is there? No answer. Only *"You will be* with me..."

Before his crucifixion, when Jesus anticipated questions about the future, he promised his followers, *"I am going to prepare a place for you... and if I go and prepare a place for you, I will come again and will take you to myself, that where I am you may be also"* (John 14:2-3 emphasis added). Though not specifying when's and where's, Jesus clearly spoke about a "place", and that place is wherever he is. He didn't elaborate further. Did he think we didn't need that information? Or did he perhaps believe we couldn't fully grasp what might be involved?

So, we turn to Paul again. In an earlier chapter of 2 Corinthians he responded to what may have been "Where?" questions. Ending chapter 4 with talk about *"our outer self...wasting away",* and our *"momentary affliction preparing for us an eternal weight of glory"* (4:16-17), he went on to write about what happens when this "earthly tent", our body, stops functioning. Again, explanations fail Paul and he has to use metaphors. We will be given a "house", an eternal house, a heavenly dwelling; we will be "clothed" with immortality (5:1,2,4). We can hear Corinthian believers asking, "But, Paul, where are those who have fallen asleep, that is, who have passed away?" And finally, he came to the answer: those who are *"absent from the body",* are *"at home with the Lord"* (2 Corinthians 5:8). With the Lord!

Where is my mother? All we have is that statement: "With the Lord". That's as far as we can go. But the statement comes as a promise. And the promise has the backing of the word of Christ. Not only his word, but his experience. He has gone before us. He has prepared a place for us to be, a place for my mother to be. That seems to be as much as Jesus wants us to know. He trusts us to trust him.

A Woman of Thankfulness

So, when the question – "Where is my mother?" – comes to mind the answer deals not so much with a "where" as with a "who". Not location but relationship. In Paul's response "With the Lord", the emphasis is on the person, the Lord. My assurance is that whatever my mother needs he is providing. She is under his attentive care.

P. T. Forsyth, an insightful theologian of the early 20th century, wrote about his mother, and mine and yours, "There are those who can quietly say, as their faith follows their [loved one] into the unseen, 'I know that land. Some of my people [my mother] live there. Some have gone abroad there on secret foreign service, which does not admit of communication. But I meet from time to time the Commanding Officer [Jesus]. And when I mention them to Him, He assures me all is well'". (From This Life and the Next)

But maybe Meister Eckhart, a 16th-century German spiritual teacher, has the better perspective when he writes: "God is at home. We are in the far country." My mother is at home. Your mother is at home. Jesus is home.

46.
WORSHIP IN THE YARD

How rich to sit here listening to wren-music, watching the morning sun patch the landscape with checkered light and shadow. To have eyes bathed with colors around and in front – yellow primrose, half-folded for the night, awaiting their full entrance into the day. There, blue-spiked delphiniums, stand proudly against the green, ever-blazing geraniums, which are never ashamed to out-dazzle the ferns and variegated hostas. Those pink-red begonias low to the ground, eager to break out and flow over the whole flower bed.

A bunny scampers over the grass, anxious about enemies. The trickling of the water fountain presents background music for a pink impatiens song, proclaiming their glory.

A flitting butterfly feasts on nectar. And having just read Psalm 24, waves of melody from "Messiah" – *"Who is this King of glory? The Lord strong and mighty! He is the King of glory!"* (vs. 10) – carry me into fitting worship. This King of greater glory – to whom belong all wrens, delphiniums, primroses, suns, spruce, impatiens and perky squirrels playing tag in the cottonwood tree. *"The earth is the Lord's and everything in it..."* *"The whole earth is full of his glory"* (Psalm 24:1; Isaiah 6:3). And thus, I worship and praise and bless you, O Lord!

47.
SHAMELESS IMPUDENT PRAYER – Luke 11:1-13

"Now Jesus was praying in a certain place, and when he finished, one of his disciples said to him, 'Lord, teach us to pray, as John taught his disciples… And he said to them, 'Which of you who has a friend will go to him at midnight and say to him, "Friend, lend me three loaves, for a friend of mine has arrived on a journey, and I have nothing to set before him"; and he will answer from within, "Do not bother me; the door is now shut, and my children are with me in bed. I cannot get up and give you anything"? I tell you, though he will not get up and give him anything because he is his friend, yet because of his impudence he will rise and give him whatever he needs. And I tell you, ask, and it will be given to you; seek, and you will find; knock, and it will be opened to you. For everyone who asks receives, and the one who seeks finds, and to the one who knocks it will be opened. What father among you, if his son asks for a fish, will instead of a fish give him a serpent; or if he asks for an egg, will give him a scorpion? If you then, who are evil, know how to give good gifts to your children, how much more will the heavenly Father give the Holy Spirit to those who ask him!"

Jesus' viewed one aspect of prayer as being earnestly persistent. HeHe used a mini-parable to illustrate such persistence: a man going to his neighbor in the middle of the night to get bread for a guest. Finding the neighbor reluctant to get out of bed, the man kept pounding on the door until his request was granted. The King James Version (KJV) in verse 8 uses the word "importunity", which carries the idea of being tenacious. The Greek word supports this sense, even to the point of being obnoxiously bold or impudent. We might even use the phrase "being in your face". The man Jesus described acted "shamelessly", another nuance of the word "persistent". He was not embarrassed to stand outside his friend's home and bang noisily on the door, perhaps waking other neighbors in the process. He didn't care what anyone else thought. He wanted bread; he knew his friend had bread, and he insisted on getting bread. His guest was in need.

The passage began with disciples asking Jesus to teach them to pray. He offered a short version of what we call the Lord's Prayer. But then Jesus continued his teaching on prayer with this emphasis on persistence. Can we assume that Jesus himself prayed to the Father in this fashion? But the question naturally arises: Why would the Son of God need to "bang on the Father's door" persistently, impudently? Would not his requests have been met with quick responses? Persistence implies a waiting, an extended time period in which the request is repeated. Why would Jesus need to wait for his Father to answer, and to keep posing his request over and over? Certainly, there is mystery involved here.

Nevertheless, in contrast to this parable, much praying lacks the intensity Jesus pictures. Many prayers tend to be rather pallid stuff. The passion required for this kind of persistent prayer signals that what one is praying about really, really matters. And what really matters has to grip a person's heart. The question is, How does one get to that point?

Maybe a line by the 19th century P. T. Forsythe can help us: "Failure to pray is a failure to discern – to discern what really matters, and to discern who really rules." (The Soul of Prayer)

48.
YOU ARE!

"You Are!" These short two words have significance in an approach to Jesus. The human mind cannot cross easily to the reality of Jesus in a spiritual realm. When I reach out, grasping for reality in relation to Christ, these two words capture a great amount of truth. When I want to really know him, I can speak these words with confidence. How can a person break beyond seeing "*through a glass dimly*" (1 Corinthians 13:12)? These two simple words "You Are" seem to help. There is no elaboration on all Jesus' characteristics, which most Christians can recite endlessly. No theological exposition attends them. The statement simply acknowledges him and his being there. He himself can fill in the details if he so wills.

It's quite different from an equally short statement: "He Is!". Such is a declaration of believing about his existence, or believing his activity in history and even now. The "You Are!" becomes a direct expression addressed to Christ himself. The two short words are a prayer.

Speaking to Jesus in this way relieves me of trying to figure out and analyze a lot of truth that may apply to one's current circumstances. There are of course other times to do that, times of intense study of Scripture, of deep meditation.

The two words build confidence the more they are expressed. When my thoughts turn to Jesus, I can say with faith, "You Are!" And maybe that's enough. In some situations, that's all that needs to be said.

It becomes my morning declaration upon waking!